Mystic Journey to India

The Key to Spiritual Awakening and Fixing Fate.

NOW AN INTERNATIONAL TV SERIES

CRAIG HAMILTON-PARKER

CRAIG HAMILTON-PARKER

"Mind-Boggling!"

Following his seminal book *'Messages from the Universe'* Craig Hamilton-Parker continues his mystical quest to discover the secrets of destiny and thereby change its course. He encounters the 10,000 year old Naadi Oracle of India that holds the mind boggling secrets that will change the course of your life.

'Mystic Journey to India' tells of Craig's incredible exploration of hidden India where he meets astrologers, strange holy men and mystics to learn their secrets and apply the spiritual remedies needed to influence the course of his life and fate.

Craig Hamilton-Parker hails from a spiritualist background and is one of the UK's most famous mediums. With the knowledge he has gained about western mysticism and mediumship he sets out on a pioneering spiritual adventure to bridge the spiritual teachings of East and West. He presents the reader with inspired ideas that are formative, groundbreaking and original.

'Mystic Journey to India' is now an International Television series and available for download.

Copyright © 2016 Craig Hamilton-Parker
www.psychics.co.uk
craig@psychics.co.uk

All rights reserved.

ISBN-13: 978-1974280872
ISBN-10: 197428087X

Celebrity Testimonials

"I don't normally buy this stuff. I think it's odd and peculiar and you can't really put your finger on this kind of thing, however – both these people – everything they said about the stuff they talked about, they were accurate. They are the real deal and it kinda blew my mind a little bit. I'm not a mind blower by nature but you know it was real and, all crap aside, it was real."

ERIC ROBERTS
(Talking to camera about his reading with Craig & Jane)

Eric Anthony Roberts is an American actor. His career began with King of the Gypsies, earning a Golden Globe Award nomination for Best Actor Debut. He earned both a Golden Globe and Academy Award nomination for his supporting role in Runaway Train

"That was remarkable...In the World's Most Skeptical Person's Award in 2001 I was a runner up but I just don't know what to make of what I've just seen. I think he did remarkably well!"

CHRIS PACKHAM
(Talking on BBC 'Inside Out' about Craig's psychic demonstration)

Christopher Gary "Chris" Packham is an English television presenter.

Contents

1	**What is the purpose of this birth?** The 10,000 year old Naadi Oracle reveals the path	1
2	**Glimpses of Higher Truth** New secrets of the oracle are revealed.	15
3	**We are the Architect of our own Destiny** Can we control our destiny and karma?	20
4	**Mystic Journey to India** Can we make this into a film?	29
5	**Spirit of Adventure** The adventures of my grandfathers.	34
6	**Tuning in to India** Tuning in to India using psychometry.	40
7	**Ancient Thiruvannamali** The strange influences of the sacred mountain.	56
8	**Ramana Maharshi** Who am I? Ancient messages from the saint.	72
9	**David Godman** Interview about the nature of the Self.	79
10	**The Siddha Yogis** The miracles of the deathless yogis.	86
11	**Ramalinga Swamigal** The man who could turn into light.	100
12	**Strange Remedies & Rituals** Feeling weird as the rituals take effect.	109
13	**Mysterious Temples** Strange magic rituals to unfamiliar gods.	117

14	**Mystic Mangroves** Spiritual insights in the peace of nature.	125
15	**Physical Mediumship** Exposing the spiritual cheats.	130
16	**Bhrigu Rishi Records** Vedic astrological oracle reveals more.	
17	**Naadi Shocks** Incredible new messages from the ancient sages.	150
18	**Heaven and Reincarnation** Do we go to Heaven or Reincarnate?	163
19	**Appendix** The Naadi transcripts in detail	170
20	**Tips about Finding a Naadi Reader** Difficult Indian words explained.	200
21	**Glossary** Indian and Sanskrit words explained.	207
22	**Mantras** Chants to advance and protect your spirit	211

CRAIG & JANE HAMILTON-PARKER

Craig and Jane Hamilton-Parker
Psychic Mediums

CHAPTER 1

ॐ

What is the purpose of this birth?

Thoughts have an incredible power. Within us they are like magnets that attract other thoughts and together move as a stream of live vibrations to create what we know as the mind. Every thought we seed pulls others towards it that together build in power to make our lives a place of joy or gloom. Our minds are energetic places that we must tend with great care to ensure that life affirming and joyful thoughts may bloom, unencumbered by the weight of wrong thinking and dreary feelings. If we take care of our thoughts through spiritual practice and determination, and refuse the entry of cumbersome dark ideas, then our inner world will shine with the light of happiness. If we allow the sunshine of the soul to illuminate the inner world then the troubles that beset us from without have less power over the course of our life.

We psychics also say that thoughts extend beyond the fabric of the brain and reach out into the world to touch the people around us. This is why psychics and mediums can pick up the thoughts of other people and sense the thoughts of the beings in the spirit world. Some mystics argue that everything that exists is a manifestation of thought and that even the physical world is an objectification of our inner world. If we could but realize the power of our thoughts then we could simply imagine the world into a better form.

Many people today buy into the idea that thoughts can influence the world around us. The attractive power of thought draws positive and negative things into our lives and has the miraculous power to change the course of events. A great deal is made of this by advocates of positive thinking who claim that we can totally change our lives simply by thinking in positive ways. We see this law at work in our lives and may notice that it's possible to think oneself into sickness or health or attract or repel good fortune by our thinking and attitude. All your hopes and all your fears may come true if you focus attention on them. Just as we are shaped by our thoughts and feelings so too these also shape the world around us.

These ideas are only part of the solution to finding a happy life. The idea – that we become what we think – ties in with the western preoccupation with the intellect and the idea that we can change our lives through visualizing wealth and so on. The positive thinking industry is in some ways a flawed philosophy that taps into greedy thinking masked by terms such as 'attracting abundance', self-empowerment and so on. The lifestyle gurus miss the point in that it is the *compassionate* thoughts we project that have the most influence on our present life and future conditions. Compassion is the antidote to karma and all types of wrong thinking. Engaging the heart through compassion is the magic medicine that cures all ills. Simply thinking positive thoughts will not work on its own and may lead to disappointment, exhaustion and a few rich authors.

Our words, actions, character, and heart create karma as do our thoughts, feelings and intent. We are creating karma now and we have created karma in the past and in our past lives. While it is true that our thoughts can influence our world and the future, the effects of our past life actions nonetheless fly towards us like an arrow that has left the bow and may cut us down with illness and misfortune. This is why bad things may happen to good people, for the negative effects of their sins from former lives are now playing out in the present. Prayer and positive thinking can help a person through but the arrow strikes and they fall. Surely, if we could somehow clear the dark clouds of past karma then wouldn't the sun be free to shine by itself? But how can we do this? How can we remove karma's negative effects and find our way?

Some heavy karma hit me at the age of 60. My internet business had been doing well but overnight Google made an algorithm change which meant that traffic to my website went from millions of visitors to a trickle. The articles that I'd written on my website over fifteen years had been copied by so many other sites that now Google saw my site as spam. Loads of sites had duplicated my content and Google's machine intelligence assumed that my site was just another rubbish site that aggregated its content from everyone else. There were other factors at play, too, but the result was that my years of exhausting work were now worthless and my income fell to near zero.

Dazed and distressed by my karmic slap round the face with a cricket bat I spent many desperate months struggling to put things back together. Meanwhile lots of other clouds filled the sky with family problems, betrayal from close friends, health concerns – lots of problems big and small cast their shadow simultaneously. The clouds were closing in and now the sky was as dark as coal.

According to Vedic traditions, karma manifests in a number of forms. What I was experiencing here is Prarabdha karma. Prarabdha means 'begun' so the effects of the karma are manifesting now. You cannot avoid or change Prarabdha karma as it is already happening. The next form of karma is Sanchita karma. Sanchita means 'gathered'. It is the karma that we have brought with us. This type of karma can be cleared through spiritual practices such as yoga, meditation, prayers, pilgrimage, keeping good company and service to others. And finally there is Agami karma, which means 'not come'. This is the karma that will take effect in the future. It is determined by your actions, thoughts and intents made in this life.

The Prarabdha karma that had hit me had to be endured but there is a factor that can override all of the above and that is grace. In my case the grace came in the form of a dream of the Indian teacher Sathya Sai Baba who appeared in my lucid dream about the holy Indian city of Varanasi. Over and over he asked me in the dream "Why are you here, why are you here, why are you here?" I had no idea. The dream had many potential meanings but was the trigger for a series of strange and fortuitous events that eventually brought me to consult an ancient Indian oracle called the Naadi. The above story, and the mind-boggling revelations made by the oracle, form the basis of my other book titled *Messages from the Universe*.

I felt that the dream and subsequent revelations in the oracle were God's way of giving me the opportunity to change my destiny through self-effort. We are all, at some time in our lives, given a chance to grow closer to the divine – that is everyone's destiny – but whether we answer the call or how far we go on this quest is in our own hands and the results are determined by our own striving.

The oracle was mind-bogglingly accurate about my life to date and made astonishing predictions about my future. What I was told shook me deeply as I had gone to great lengths to ensure that the separate *readers*, whom I consulted, would have absolutely no idea of who I was or be given any clues to allow them to check me out on the Internet. It revealed the history of my life, described my previous incarnations and told me what I must do in this life now to fulfil my personal destiny. At last I knew the purpose of my birth and had found a way to help others to discover theirs.

Getting Proof

I explained in *Messages to the Universe* how I went to great lengths to ensure that the *readers* did not know anything about who I was. They were not even given my name – in fact all *readers* were given was my thumbprint and, from this, they found the appropriate leaf bundles in which my personal Naadi leaf was found. These readers held separate Naadi bundles yet all told a similar story about my life history and predicted very similar things about my future. They revealed different past lives, as did the new readings that I will mention later in this book.

Consulting the oracle is done in three stages. The first step is to find the leaf bundle that contains your personal leaf. This is done from the thumbprint but it is not always possible to find your leaf as the British destroyed some of the leaves at the time of the Raj. Once the thumbprint identifies the correct bundle the *reader* goes through the leaves one by one in a process of elimination until a leaf that corresponds to you is found. So, in my case, the *reader* asked questions such as 'Do you import precious metals?' If my answer is 'no' the leaf is discarded and we move on the next one. This can take hours but, in my case, the leaf was found within about twenty minutes. The questions were not leading questions that would help the *reader* to make a guess about me but odd questions like the one I have just cited.

After discarding about ten leaves the readers asked me "Is your ex-wife's name Tina?" I nearly fell off my chair because she is not someone I have named in any of my books and there is nothing published on the Internet or elsewhere. It would have taken quite a lot of research to get to that quickly – and remember the readers were not even given my name. All they had was a thumb print and nothing else before seeing me face-to-face by Skype. Again I have addressed these issues in detail in my earlier book.

Incredibly the *reader* then told me that my mother's name is Ethel, (not a common name today) my father's name was Donald and that he used to work as a rent collector as a young man (most members of my family don't know that); that I had one brother who was married and a sister who is a widow (all correct). He said that my present wife's name is Jane and that, like me, she has a spiritual consultancy business but our businesses are separate. (Jane is self-employed but I run my work as a limited company. He would have needed our tax records to know that.) All of this he simply read from the leaf and I would only answer yes or no. If I forgot myself and tried to be helpful with a pronunciation of a name (He struggles a bit with Donald) he would stop me and insist I only give yes/no answers and he must just read what it says on the leaf. "You were born on the 24th January 1954. This was a Sunday and you were born at 1:30 am in the morning." By now I was visible shocked and shaking like a leaf. In the tone of someone revealing a great secret, he made the big reveal and said: "Your name is Craig!"

There were many more things he had to say about my life and past that nobody could possibly have known or looked up on the Internet and, again, I have given full details about these in my earlier book. I have explained there how I used a proxy to ensure that no details about me could be looked up or researched on the Internet and that no cold reading techniques were being used. I was also conscious of the trickery that the skeptics highlight and of how human psychology is prone to believe what it wants to believe. For example skeptics talk about the Barnum effect, also called the Forer effect, which is the observation that individuals will give high accuracy ratings to descriptions of their personality that supposedly are tailored specifically for them but are, in fact, vague and general enough to apply to a wide range of people. I know about all of this but the proofs that the first Naadi reader gave were so astonishing that it felt that reality was caving in. It was completely mind-boggling.

I am no stranger to the paranormal as, for most of my life, I have been working as a professional psychic medium. My wife Jane is also a psychic medium and together we have tried to give solid proof of the continuation of life after death by proving the reality of the next world and thereby give lasting comfort and solace to the bereaved. We have seen and experienced some amazing real phenomena but also know how to spot a fake. What I was witnessing with the Naadis was real.

After the predictions have been made, the Naadi gives a series of remedies that must be performed to eradicate the negative effects of the Sanchita karma that will come in the future. You can either do the remedies yourself – which is recommended - – or have the Naadi reader commission a Brahman priest to do them by proxy. In my previous book I describe how I had a few of the remedies done for me but did most of the remedies myself by visiting Hindu Temples around the UK.

There remained a number of remedies that could not be done properly without visiting India and you will soon read about my journey to India to do these odd remedies by visiting holy people and places, doing special rituals and undertaking charitable acts to push my destiny onto a new course. I am also using the story of this strange spiritual adventure to teach you some of the basics about Indian mysticism and western mediumship and to discover the answers to life's big questions and the purpose of human life. I include known philosophy as well as new revelations from the mystic masters that have remained undisclosed for centuries. In effect, what I am doing through these magical rituals is changing the course of my life and steering my destiny to a safe shore. I am fixing fate.

I've been a psychic medium all of my life but the Naadis had opened me to something that was incomprehensible. Deep down inside I knew that something was missing and now ancient India was calling me again to find out her most hidden secrets. I felt that I was standing on the edge of a phenomenon which was much greater than what I was able to access by mediumship or other spiritual means, so now I went in search of what that thing is and, by extension, in search of my true self.

In my first book about the Naadi I told the story of the oracles' revelations and intertwined stories from my life as a psychic medium and as part of a psychic family. I wrote about the philosophy of karma and enlightenment as well as the spiritual implications of knowing the future – including the significance of being told the time I will die.

Soon we will begin the story of my journey to India to do the 'remedies' prescribed by the oracle to enhance or negate the effects of my past life karma. We will visit mystical places and meet holy people who guide me on my path and reveal to me extraordinary things about the nature of existence and the purpose of human life but first, for those who have not read my first book, let me tell you a little more about this remarkable oracle, the mysteries that surround it and the dangers of being led astray.

The Ancient Oracle

The Naadi oracle is written on palm leaves that have been carbon dated to between 200 and 400 years of age. They are copies of older leaves that have been copied and recopied for thousands of years. The oracle says that my own leaves were written in a time period called the Dwapara Yuga that, according to the saintly astrologer Swami Sri Yukteswar, who was the guru of the famous spiritual master Paramahansa Yogananda, ran from 3100 BC until 700 BC.

The Naadi oracle is so mind-boggling with the accuracy of its readings that I'm inclined to believe that it must have been written by people with some form of super-consciousness who had the ability to see far into the future. These archaic people had powers of clairvoyance that modern man finds hard to imagine. Today our lives look outward to the objective world and we live by rationality, reason and science but many legends tell that there was a time long-ago when people had mastered their inner world and could use the energy connected to consciousness to manipulate the physical world and gain knowledge of the secrets of the universe through direct intuitive knowledge. They could see into infinite space and time.

The Age of Dwapara Yuga ended at the 'death' of Krishna who withdrew from this world 36 years after the great battle of Mahabharata – which some historians say is a myth – but astronomy and astrological references in various holy texts suggest happened sometime between 3102 BC and 3067 BC. The Puranic text called the *Bhagavata Purana* says that the Dwapara Yuga lasts 864,000 years.

Whatever way you look at it, the Naadi oracles claim to be very old indeed and some say that the prophecies may have been written down at a time that could pre-date archeological records: perhaps even passed to us from a spiritually advanced people who lived before the last Ice Age. Many archeologists are claiming that the history of civilization is far older than we have ever imagined and the writing from the Naadi may be the last traces of this great civilization.

Mainstream archeology's assumptions about the history of humankind are now being challenged and it seems that civilization has been here much longer than we have anticipated. Seeds have been found which show that ancient man was planting cultivated grains 23,000 years ago. Excavations at Gobekli Tepe in Turkey have recently revealed a series of 12,000-year-old megalithic stone circles that are larger and more complex than Stonehenge in England and are 7,000 years older. The Egyptian Sphinx was carved over 7,000 years ago, or more, and the pyramids are some of the most accurately constructed buildings in the world; yet all of this was done when human civilization was just getting started. And Sanskrit – the language in which the Naadi leaves were first written – can be traced back 9,000 years and yet is considered by linguists to be the most complete and well-structured language ever devised. It strikes me that ancient peoples were highly sophisticated and that we have lost a great deal of an ancient knowledge during the spiritually dark times from which we are now emerging.

The mystics in the East believe that, pre-dating the Dwapara Yuga, there were two other great ages called Treta Yuga and Satya Yuga when humankind had super-human spiritual powers and a transcendental consciousness which could foresee the future of all beings. The Yugas turn like a great wheel and, right now, we are leaving a time of materialism and ignorance called Kali Yuga and in the process of entering a better age. As we do this, there will be some problems for the world but with the change in times also comes the return of the lost knowledge of the ancient past, for spiritual truth is like mathematics: no matter how much of it is lost, it can always be rediscovered.

Thinking Differently

The knowledge passed down in the Naadis is not the type of knowledge that you may be used to. It is a form of knowledge that comes from a time when people thought in a different way and had a sense of intuitive involvement with the universe. Mystics argue that, before the dominance of reasoning, we had the power to know things instantly through direct experience in a similar way to how an idiot savant is able to recognize if a huge number is a prime or not. This ability would require complex calculations, because no simple algorithms are known for determining primes, and yet these savants simply know the answers without understanding how they do it. In a similar way, the knowledge of the ancients was a 'received knowledge' that, perhaps, tapped into a quantum level of consciousness and gave direct realization of the secrets of existence. In the Golden Age, which the Naadi oracles sometimes speak about, people learnt by direct insight rather than by assimilating information as we do today.

In the pages ahead I will be explaining how the Naadi leaves foresee our destiny but also are a personalized guide to enlightenment that directly opens us to the ancient knowledge. I will be telling you about the magical remedies, mantras and rituals which were prescribed by the oracle for my spiritual progress and how these triggered an inner transformation and changed the course of events that were yet to happen. We will be looking way into the distant past and far ahead into the distant future of mankind.

The inner revolution that happened to me is not something that happens to everyone who consults the leaves but, if the right person makes a consultation at the right time in their life, the oracle can rapidly propel their spiritual progress. Although the oracle is today generally used for fortune telling, I believe its hidden remit is to transform our inner world and awaken our higher consciousness. The ancient seers knew that mankind today would get into trouble through its rational materialism so gave us a way to rediscover the lost knowledge of the spirit.

Although the oracle was written thousands of years ago, it feels like a living energy that thinks for itself and serves as a live communication with the great sages of the past who have insight into the present moment. These great seers knew what questions we would ask centuries before we were born. They even knew the exact moment when we would open the leaves for a consultation. They could anticipate my writing this book and your reading it and see those of you who will seek to consult the oracle in the future as well as those who will find it and those who will fail.

What the oracle said to me was exceptional but it is very

important to remember that the vast majority of the Naadi readers in India – and particularly on the Internet – are complete frauds. Do not be taken in. I will detail this later and will draw your attention to this again and again. In addition, even the *readers* who are sincere can make mistakes and it seems that even the slightest wrong motive can cause the predictions to go awry, for the oracle is influenced by the thoughts and ambitions of both the *reader* and the person consulting the oracle. Even the spiritually minded readers whom I've met can easily fall from the path for we live in the dark age of Kali Yuga and its materialistic shadows can easily be cast on the proceedings. There are some *readers* whom I once trusted who now overcharge for their services so that their oracle is now no longer pure or accurate. The leaves themselves will stop giving clear information to a Naadi reader who has fallen from grace.

All this will sound like nonsense at first but, once you have made multiple consultations with the real oracle, you will see that it knows about future events in great detail and also knows about what you've done since the last consultation and what remedies you have completed – even when you are talking to completely different *readers*. It gets really spooky sometimes as it is like speaking directly to the long dead Maharishis who wrote the text all those centuries ago.

Cheating Scumbags

I am outspoken when I meet scam artists and cheats and am often appalled by the stupidity, egotism, low moral standards and trickery that I have seen in my fellow mediums and psychics. Sadly, genuine mediums become guilty by association and I can understand why many people dismiss all psychics and mediums as crackpots and money mad fraudsters. And so it is with the Naadi readers in India for there's a huge number of fakes claiming to be custodians of genuine leaves but, in reality, only one in ten thousand are true – it's got that bad so watch out!

A false Naadi reader will use the leaf finding process as a way to extract information about you. As there are traditionally 108 leaves in each bundle and three bundles are usually used then this means that in some cases questioning can go on for hours with hundreds of questions asked. The *reader* will ask confusing questions mixed with targeted questions used to get the information from you that he needs. Once your name, date of birth, place of birth and time of birth have been identified then they have enough information to make your astrological chart using traditional Indian Astrology. The reading you are given is simply an astrological reading.

I recorded my own leaf finding process, in all cases, and I am sure that they could not have found the information they required from my guarded 'yes' and 'no' responses. Similarly with others I've helped to find their leaves; we have checked everything meticulously and watched our responses to ensure that nothing was being given away. Critics argue that what makes Naadi Astrology appear more authentic is that they provide you with a lot of information about your family, your background, your profession, career aspirations and so on. They claim that these details are given to the astrologer by the person during the leaf finding process. This is probably the case in many instances but was definitely not the case for the people I've worked with. Again, I have gone into detail, about the many safeguards I put in place to stop this happening, in my earlier book.

I have friends in India who are working on an antidote to these poisonous purveyors of false prophecy by encouraging *readers* to work for free and leave it to the person making the consultation to give a non-obligatory donation if they feel inclined. This is how the original Naadis worked and, by taking away the greed element, it purifies motive and releases a spiritual power that facilitates 100% accuracy to the readings. To consult the oracle with bad intent, revenge, personal gain, and so on will backfire, as abridged Tamil script written in fading miniscule letters can easily be misread and misinterpreted, for the oracle is like a living being that may decide to shield or withhold the truth from wrong minded people. Some say that the words, on the Jeeva Naadi in particular, have often been seen to physically change on the leaf as a question is being asked. The oracle re-writes itself! It is clear that these miraculous things have to be approached with care, and with the purest spiritual purpose, if absolute clarity is to be obtained from the oracle.

The Naadi made many accurate observations and predictions about my life, and correctly foresaw a number of events that happened since my last book, but further enquiries to the oracle have it urging me to make the best of my karma and do more of the prescribed remedies. The remedies are things such as healing mantras to overcome future illness, temple rituals to be done at specific places and times, and charitable acts to the poor. All this will ensure a bright future and negate the negative effects of past karma.

Paying for Remedies by Proxy

You can pay the Naadi readers and Brahmin priests to do the remedies on your behalf but it is generally advised that it is much better to do them for yourself. At the conclusion of my first book I had commissioned a few remedies that were impossible to achieve outside of India and had visited temples in the UK to perform what I could of the list of remedies written in my leaves and had chanted the prescribed mantras for hundreds of hours.

Of course there is no obligation whatsoever to do any of these remedies and the sceptic will says it's a load of hocus-pocus anyway but my reasoning was that if an oracle could be so tremendously accurate about my past and present life then its predictions for the future should be listened to very carefully. And if there are magical remedies that can be performed to smooth the way then it seemed to me to be circumspect to do them. The limited remedies I'd been able to do had left me with a hard-to-describe feeling of release and an influx of positive energy to my life. My mind may rebel at all this apparent nonsense but my heart and my health were telling me that these remedies were certainly doing something transformative to me on an energetic level.

Getting proof from the Naadis is in some ways the same as having proof of mediumship. When I first started looking into it, I met many seemingly honest practitioners who were not in the slightest way gifted. I'd met trance mediums who spewed out ridiculous psychobabble that allegedly came from highly advanced spiritual beings; I'd seen people channel aliens and talk in high squeaky voices about lizard beings; I'd been told the colours of my aura without any collaborating proofs of what it means; I'd been told wild things about my past lives and spirit guides and had daft messages from all sorts of 'psychic' people who gave no verifiable proofs. I'm sure you've encountered these people for they are everywhere and their misguided foolishness eclipses the true work being done by the very, very few real mediums alive today.

When you are given evidence from a real medium it can be like a hammer blow to skepticism. In my case it was the medium Doris Stokes from Grantham who not only gave amazing verifications and proofs of survival from my grandparents and others but even foresaw when I'd meet my future wife. "You will meet your new wife on the 6th March," she said. 'Her name will be Jane Wallis." I met my wife Jane on the 6th March nine years later whilst I was giving a demonstration of mediumship at a Spiritualist church. I was giving a public spirit message to Jane in the audience from her grandmother who, I said, was Ethel Wallis. Jane's name at the time was Jane Willis – not Wallis as Doris Stokes had said – but clearly this was very, very close and enough to make my head spin. This type of evidence that has happened time and again throughout my life gives a body of evidence that, when taken as a whole, gives irrefutable proof of life after death.

I also now know for certain that the future can be predicted as, through my work as a psychic medium, I have made thousands of highly accurate predictions that have come true. They have been verified by my personal clients and reaffirms my faith in my own abilities. I have also predicted world events that have come true and have also been given accurate predictions by other mediums and psychics that have come true to the letter.

But the Naadi goes one step further for it not only sees the future but also shows us how to influence it – not just through foresight and sensible decision-making – but by cutting out the very root of the bad karma that is causing the problem in the first place. How the Naadi writers came up with the things they say on the leaves may never be explained for we are talking here about super-human forms of clairvoyance. Similarly, it is impossible fully to understand why they give the remedies and why they work. From the standpoint of health there may be an element of the placebo effect in doing some of these things and the power of thoughts combined with trust and belief may have incredible powers too. In normal thinking, we wrap our thoughts in words but when we wrap thoughts in magical mantras they take on a new power that may fly out from us to make incredible things happen. You may be naturally skeptical about some of these ideas but it is my opinion that these extremely complex religious remedies have a real effect upon destiny that is beyond our usual criteria of comprehension. It is not until you directly experience the Naadis and set out to change fate that you can feel the eerie power of these things envelop your world. Like the White Queen in 'Alice through the Looking Glass' by Lewis Carroll, I sometimes feel that I've believed as many as six impossible things before breakfast. But the world we see is not what we think it is, for the impossible is possible.

I had decided that the knowledge given by the Naadis was a gift from the gods and I would implement and finish the remaining remedies that the oracle had revealed. I had made a good start but it was now clear that I must go to India to complete my task.

CHAPTER 2

ॐ

Glimpses of Higher Truth

"Sometimes I think you are completely mad, Craig," said Jane when I told her that I'd been on Skype and consulted the Naadi Oracles. "The only clairvoyance these people have is to have seen you coming. They just look things up on the Internet and Facebook and then feed it all back to you. Some of these people are about as psychic as a rice pudding. They don't have a gift like you and me and they are just out to fleece people."

But Jane's skeptical tone began to change when I showed her the recordings and typed transcripts. I explained the rigorous safeguards that my friend Vivek and I had put in place to ensure no cheating went on and she could see by my face pallor that I was visibly shocked by it all. I was dead serious. I showed her what the general kandams (chapters) had revealed and how the leaves had given the exact names and birth times and dates of the family. How did they know my first wife's name was Tina and how did they know all these things about our lives such as how we run separate businesses, my books, our work on TV, how we were setting up a TV production company, and how did it know the personal things about our family life and the lives of our parents and children. But, as it is with these things, it takes something seemingly insignificant but highly personal to flick the switch. "How on earth did he know I have a rash on my leg!" gasped Jane when this information was given – something that I didn't even know about until that day. And there was so much more: fact after fact proved how it would have been impossible to get any of this through an Internet search and remembering, of course, that they didn't even know my name until the reading was over.

Those wise people who have read my first book will know all this, of course, but even now, after some years have now passed since my initial consultations, I still find it all hard to believe. These first encounters with the Naadi Palm Leaf Oracle were to open the general chapters – called kandams – which 'saw' the history of my life and spoke about my previous life as rishi (spiritual person). They seemed to know everything that's important about my present life my future life and my former lives.

All of this was revealed in these General Kandams that I had consulted through three different readers in three different parts of India. Although these were different leaves from different Naadi libraries they said very similar things about my past life, my life now and my life in the future. It was hard to comprehend how three different sources could all support one another and give such powerful verification of their authenticity. As evidence they provided me with correct birth dates and times, family names and many detailed facts about my life. And all of them also gave similar prophecies for my future.

I had read the first chapters and now, of course, I was keen to know more and open other chapters from this amazing manuscript. The General Kandam serves as a summary of a person's life and will give the name of the person making the consultation and how long they will live. It also reveals information about their identity and the course of their life together with the most significant things that have already happened to them. It will give the name of their spouse, parents, children and siblings and gives details about the seeker's past and present profession. In this Kandam the exact time and date of their birth is written and, from the resulting horoscope, a summary of future predictions is given for all the 12 houses in his/her horoscope based on the planetary positions at the time of their birth.

This all sounds rather marvelous and the casual reader may think that, like some bogus tarot readers, they will fish for information by asking leading questions, tricking the sitter to offer information about themselves or giving back information that you mentioned earlier in the reading. Just as there are many suspect psychics, there are also many suspect Naadi readers but, in my case and in the cases of some of my friends and family, the Naadi readers were very precise and went straight to the information without hesitation. There was no fishing for information. The readings were straight to the point and names and details were simply read from the leaves.

Opening Other Kandams

Depending on from which Naadi library you source the palm leaves there are usually additional kandams to the main general kandam. These cover specific areas of your life and can include questions about specific aspects of your life such as childbirth, education, wealth, relationships, marriage and health. The one that most interested me was my Gnana Kandam, which deals with spiritual knowledge and the path to liberation. I was warned that not everyone has this chapter in their leaves and I may never find it.

To access this I called on the second Naadi reader, whom I spoke about in my first book, and, to my delight, he was able to find the chapter and have it translated onto an audio file and sent to me by email. The Guna Kandam confirmed and elaborated on the things that had been said in the other readings by him and other Naadi readers. The reading is from the leaves of the rishi Sat Guru Sri Agurum, transcribed thousands of years ago by Shiva Vakyaha Maharishi and presented to me as a conversation between Lord Shiva and the goddess Parvati who asks about when and how I will get spiritual knowledge (Gnana).

Again I am told that my spiritual abilities will increase and I will use these to help people. I will use my spiritual powers – which I broadly understand as my mediumistic powers – for the welfare of the world. I am told that this Gnana Kandam is very rare and can only be accessed once you have attained a degree of spiritual growth. Again it confirmed that the leaf is mine by citing the correct name of my father and mother and that I'd be listening to the reading at the age of 62 (61 running).

I have included the full reading in the appendix but, in brief, it tells me that I will devote myself to spiritual things and meet holymen who will further help me with my spiritual mission. By the age of 66 I will have a high degree of spiritual illumination. (I'm 62 at the time of writing this which is 63 or 62 running in the Tamil way of describing age.) It also re-confirms predictions made in my previous consultations including the fact that I will build ashrams and be able to foresee calamities and help people to avoid them. All very heady stuff that left me inspired to move forward but also perplexed as to how I could ever accomplish so much.

Destiny Waits

It was clear to me that sitting at home waiting for things to happen spontaneously was not an option as I developed a growing feeling of frustration that I may not be able to fulfil my destiny. The Naadis had given me a long list of spiritual remedies to perform to reduce the negative effects of my past karma and to clear the way for the future. I had done many of these at Hindu temples in the UK, and had some performed on my behalf by proxy, but there were many rituals and ceremonies that would be hard to do outside of India.

"Jane, do you fancy doing a holiday in India? It would be so interesting and I could see if I can do these final remedies. I'm sure you'll love it. Money is still tight so we'd probably have to fly economy class."

"Do I look like an economy type of girl?" she retorts. "I don't do economy. I'm allergic to economy." Then a little more seriously she added "No I really don't feel that this is for me. This Naadi thing is your path. I know where I'm going from what the spirits tell me. Last time we went to India to see Sai Baba was hard enough. Driving hundreds of miles in broken down old taxis on dirt tracks with everyone clambering to get my baggage nearly did me in. You said the hotel in Bangalore would be nice and what did I get? There were rats as big as dogs running up the walls and waiters who picked their noses as they served us food. I wanted to see Sai Baba but this one has to be your adventure."

I had read that it is far better to perform remedial ceremonies in person and was coming to the conclusion that there was really no course other than for me to go to India.

"I have absolutely no problem with you going if you want to. Leave me enough money and bring me back something nice and I'm happy."

Jane was giving me the green light but the idea of visiting the depths of India on my own and working out how to do these elaborate rituals was a huge wall before me. My worry was that I had no contacts in India to help me and the Naadi leaves had given me a list of temples to visit that were scattered over thousands of miles in obscure locations. I'd been told to seek out holy-men, do fire rituals and get blessings at places that were very remote. Who would show me where to go, how to approach the holy men or what to do in the temples?

"Will you be driving across India?" says Jane reading my mind. "You know what a nightmare it is. You'll have to get taxis and that will probably cost the earth!"

She was right of course. There was absolutely no way I could drive in India! I knew from my earlier visits that they drive like a Demolition Derby on potholed dirt-track roads covered with cows, kids, overloaded bullock carts, massive old British-built lorries, rickshaws, scurrying motorbikes with high-speed hand-on-the-horn mayhem everywhere. Crossing the road there is a challenge, let alone driving a car. I'm a confident driver but in India driving without dying isn't easy. Fifteen people were killed every hour in Indian road accidents during 2016; one million have died in the last decade and five million were seriously injured in a country where ambulances are in short supply. Furthermore, finding the temples with impossible-to-pronounce names and scattered over thousands of miles across Southern India would also be a major challenge.

Doing all of this on my own was just too daunting a prospect. I may have the striking good looks of a Hollywood star but I'm no Indiana Jones. I so wanted to go but maybe the time was not right. The journey had been predicted but it looked like it wasn't going to happen. Had the Maharishis, who wrote the leaves, seen all this with their celestial eyes?

"Jane I'm going to do it," I said. "I know it's a huge and dangerous step but I feel such a strong calling. India is like a magnet."

"Once you make the inner decision the path will open," replied Jane cryptically. "Let's see what happens."

CHAPTER 3

ॐ

We are the Architect of our own Destiny

My book *Messages from the Universe* raised many questions about the Naadi oracle that I was unable to answer, as reliable information is very hard to find. At times I felt that I was stumbling alone in the dark, carrying a sacred treasure that I dare not let drop from my hands. There are next-to-no books about the Naadis but I managed to buy one of the last remaining copies of Kim Paisol's book *Naadi Palmleaf Astrology* from Amazon, which gave me lots of useful information and startling examples of Naadi leaf predictions.

I was really pleased to be able to track down Kim Paisol who lives in Denmark and he was willing to make some comments about my book by email and answer my questions about the Naadi. With so few people to talk to about my discoveries it was a boon to connect with someone who had spent a large part of his life investigating the mysteries of the Naadi. Kim could answer some of the many questions I had:

Craig: Can you spot any errors in *Messages from the Universe*?

Kim: Your Naadi readings would be greatly improved if a spiritually evolved person could help you to "translate and transform" the readings you have received so far. It looks as if the first reading you had is from what is called the *Mahasiva Sukshma Naadi*. This is a detailed and elaborate Naadi reading that mostly contains information about your future on the basis of the position of Saturn, Jupiter, Raghu and Ketu's transits from the Moon in your chart. In some cases the predictions are extremely accurate and in some cases they are not. The main centre of this Naadi is in the village Vaitheesvarankoil, now with offices here and there in India.

The two different readings you had claim two different sets of thumb impressions, with different names and dots, which is not very likely unless several years have passed since the first and second reading. Also, some of the planets are not placed correctly: Sukra/Venus for instance is said to be in Sagittarius with Raghu. It is not, it's about 9 degrees in Capricorn.

Craig: So will this make a big difference to the predictions that I wrote about in my book?

Kim: There are some errors and wrong sayings in the translation of your Naadi readings but that is unfortunately quite often seen. Luckily, in your case, it may not make much difference to the inner meaning of both readings.

Craig: I am an Aquarius in the Western Astrological system yet the Naadi said I am a Capricorn. Why is this?

Kim: Indian astrology uses the Sidereal zodiac, the western uses the tropical Zodiac and the difference is measured in what is called Ayanama, a constant moving factor increasing each year, so when the Sun in the Tropical Zodiac is 10 degree Aquarius we have to subtract the Ayanamsa for the year to get the true Sidereal Zodiac and these years it is about 24 degrees, next year more and so on until 30 degrees difference, then it starts all over again. So that part should be ok.

Craig: Why do errors occur?

Kim: 99% of the Naadi readings are read by readers who are not in tune with, or who understand, the true inner spiritual meaning of the leaves and may miss what the Rishi is seeking to give you as a message that you are, at that moment, ripe to receive. For instance, nothing is coming from the Universe or conveying a message from the Universe. You *are* the Universe and the creator of what is seen or experienced. Nothing comes from outside the Self.

This is the very essence of all spiritual scriptures and the liberated ones of India. Remember, also, that nothing is ever conveyed to anyone unless they are a developed soul and ripe to receive the message. This is the philosophy I have learnt from the words of Sri Ramana Maharishi.

Craig: How is it best to approach the past life karma issues that the Naadis talk about?

Kim: There are many mundane concepts included and sometimes *readers* give wrong advice. For instance, when it says that you, in a previous birth as a woman in search of the ultimate truth, had to leave your family, then all bad comments and results follow from this action. But this is not so in India: seeking God always has been the highest purpose of life and no one is ever cursed for this. The tricky part here is that you did that as a woman and, for that alone, words such as curses and so on are used. If you did the same as a man, this would not have been written.

Craig: Do the remedies for past lives have an effect?

Kim: When the *reader* says that you have not attained a status or have the results, that as you may deserve, then this is all due to your *Prahabdha karma* and could not be otherwise.

Craig: I understand Prahabdha Karma to be karma that cannot be recalled – like an arrow fired from a bow.

Kim: You see, whatever we try to do to make things happen or whatever we try to do for things not to happen, then it will always happen in accordance with our Prahabdha karma. So we will, or will not, receive exactly what is due to us. This is very important and many *readers* do not read out this from the leaves, mostly because they do not know this simple truth or they may not feel it as so. In this way ignorance influences the reading.

Craig: So remedies won't work?

Kim: Remedies may have an effect but only in the relative mundane world but not in the highest spiritual form. Any action creates another effect and with this more karma is produced, therefore the focus shall be on the spiritual path only as this will not create any desire for any further action. If we are not the past or future or ego, then who is it that is going through what we call karma or destiny? Only he who identify with form and I/ego suffers, not he who sees beyond.

Craig: I did my own remedies and temple visits with sincerity and with awe in my heart towards what the Maharishi had instructed.

Kim: With the sincerity itself much is gained.

When we concluded our dialogue I asked Kim if he would comment on my Gnana Kandam that I had recently had translated. He suggested also that Vivek and I look into the Pothis in Andra Pradesh and the Sukar Naadi at Bangalore, which is consulted by many Sai Baba devotes. He also recommended we track down a sincere Jeeva Naadi in Tamil Nadu and one in Chennai called Kagabujandar Jeeva Naadi. For these the person has to be present and these readings cannot be done remotely.

Kim suggested that, in order to give me an opinion of the Gnana Kandam, he would access one of the Naadi readers he knew in India and we would look at the Brahma Sukshma Naadi. To do this the Naadi reader has first to open my 1st, 13th and 14th Kandam. These were the sections that I spoke about in my earlier book and would again have a slightly different interpretation for my destiny and perhaps take into account what has happened since I first made my enquiries via my friend Vivek.

The Brahma Sukshma Naadi makes no charge for the readings and it is left up to the person making the consultation to pay something or not. Once the reading is received Kim would comment on the Gnana Kandam reading I had sent him and his comment is reproduced in the appendix of this book.

Kim tells me that, in ancient time, there were no fixed fees to obtain a Naadi reading and expectation of payment is a recent addition. Kim had, in fact, opened a small centre in India from 2006 – 2011 and had offered free readings to all. As it was in the past, the seeker was free to pay or not. Kim says: "In India today only 10 out of 10,000 will offer genuine Naadi readings and all these 10 will not ask for any fee but leave it to the individual and God to handle all such matters."

For the Brahma Sukshma Naadi, I sent Kim a scan of my right thumbprint and the names of my father and mother and, if they are alive, the number of my siblings and their marital status. You will note that, for my readings in my book *Messages from the Universe,* I had sent only my thumb impression and this had been sent anonymously and by proxy by my friend Vivek so that we could be absolutely sure no cheating and Internet searches were made. Like Vivek, Kim, I felt, was a trustworthy person and, because of the safeguards I put in place for my initial readings, I am convinced that the genuine Naadi readers do not cheat. Kim had been studying the Naadis for 30-35 years so I was in safe hands.

Brahma Sukshma Naadi

My leaves were found and a short time after talking to Kim my Brahma Sukshma Naadi was sent to me by email. This Naadi reading was a lot shorter and to the point than the readings organized by Vivek that I described in my book *Messages from the Universe*. It was interesting to see a different form of presentation and translation and once again the leaves – this time via a new source that was completely unconnected to Vivek and his readers – contained remarkably similar prophecies about my life and spiritual work. How could it be that three different sets of Naadi leaves in three separate parts of India all had the same things to say?

There were a few differences too and you can compare these by reading the appendixes of my two books. In all three Naadi consultations the thumbprint names and some of the planet descriptions were different. Also in this new reading the past life information was new. You will recall that in my first book I had been a male Rishi who had had a fall out with the Temple community and in another life – again in India – I had been a woman who had left her family to seek sainthood. This time, a past life was revealed that saw me as a skeptic who challenged and disrupted the meditating cave yogis but who, in later life, reformed his ways and did a lot of charitable work.

I presume that the above are three separate past lives or could be three separate interpretations by the three maharishis. Fortunately, in all three cases I had some very good karma influencing my present life and any residual bad karma could be removed to help the positive karma flower. I feel it is enough that the Naadi had once again revealed that my life was a spiritual quest. From reading other people's predictions it is clear that the Naadis will identify the primary driving forces in people's lives. It will see if you are a businessman, an artist, musician, a homemaker and so on. What is most important to you is specifically revealed in the leaves and the reading would not fit another. I have dedicated my life to mediumship and spirituality and have let go of many worldly opportunities to seek my spiritual goals. Again the Naadi seems to have highlighted the search for divine knowledge and God-realization as my goal in this life.

Forgetting Past Lives

In most instances it is very hard to prove past lives with empirical facts and I have met many people who have based their lives on unsubstantiated beliefs in past life memories. These may arise though hypnotism, from messages given by psychics and mediums, from dreams or simply from intuition. In many cases these may be genuine insights but some glorious past lives are clearly crazy fantasy dreamed up by spiritual under-achievers.

In the Greek myths the shades of the dead will drink from the River of Lethe as the soul makes its way to the paradise of Elysium. The River of Lethe flowed through the cave of Hypnos, god of sleep, and any who drank of its waters would forget their earthly life. In the *Aeneid*, the poet Virgil writes that it is only when the dead have had their memories erased by Lethe that they may be reincarnated.

There is a reason why we drink the waters of forgetting and lose the memories of our past incarnations: if we yearn after who we were we will never achieve our true potential in this life. Fixation on the past paralyses the spirit and longing for these lost days – in this present life too – will hold us back from happiness and Self-Realization. All that has ever happened and all that will ever be flows though us in the form of karma, which morphs into our individual lives. In this whirlwind of impressions the souls of those we love and those we hate chase us into paradise and back into future lives. Who we were determines what we will become, altered only by the grace of God and our own divine willpower. If we roll with the punches from

Life's Arena and are willing to change and be transformed then all this serves to quicken our growth. By moving forward we realize that what we were does not matter much but what we can become is all important.

It is fortunate that we are born with a clean slate and we can learn new things yet draw upon those unconscious talents that follow us into this life. We are free to make new choices, meet new challenges and strive to seek our heart's desires without being inhibited by the shadows of the past.

For the spiritual aspirant, there will be times when flashes of inspiration carried forward from past lives will drive them forward. These may be directly recalled memories but, more often, an insight and inner knowing that comes as a great push from the unconscious towards spiritual advancement. The revelations from the Naadis may be an actualized unconscious revelation that are somehow clouded by the past life forgetfulness, symbolized by the Greek myths of Lethe, yet still contain the essence of what drives us over many lifetimes.

The Brahma Sukshma Naadi reaffirmed a great deal that had been said before from my other consultations. It spoke of my spiritual search and included some personal information about minor illnesses, conflicts and in deaths within my family – information that I have not included in any of my writings. For the future it also predicts a vehicle accident from which I will come to no harm and a theft from me or my family. The Naadi also reaffirmed that some people would try to blacken my good name – a warning that has appeared in all the consultations. This reading also 'saw' my books, help from VIP's, spiritual consultancy and demonstrations and – just like the other Naadis – reaffirmed that I would build an ashram. It did not foresee multiple centres around the world but spoke of new properties and hired venues.

The truth of the Naadi had already been confirmed by my efforts with Vivek to get two separate readings and compare them. In this reading I was not looking to prove the reality of the first Naadi chapter, which gives an overview of my life, but to get confirmation of the Gnana Kandam that I'd opened with Vivek's reader.

You can read both of the Kandam's in the appendix if it interests you but, in essence, this one summarized my quest for realization and that, in the coming years, my insights will mature and result in direct knowledge and higher consciousness. At the time of writing I am already deeply involved in yoga and meditation and trying hard to focus, enhance and purify my consciousness and thereby improve my mediumship.

The Ghana Kandam of the Brahma Sukshma Naadi speaks about my spiritual endeavors and warns about challenges, obstacles and people who may try to thwart my efforts. It shows how crystal clarity of awareness can be obtained and talks of the 'language of silence' that is the voice of my liberated self, guiding me towards perpetual peace, service and spiritual growth. In my next birth I am told I will live as a liberated soul with a child-like innocence that can heal the sorrows of those who come to me.

I hope that my destiny will follow along the lines of this and the other Naadis' predictions but the text again points to remedies that need to be undertaken to clear the karma. It recognizes that I had already started these remedies, which I have described in *Messages from the Universe,* but suggested that these remedies were incomplete. As with the other Naadis, it urged me to go to India but now a spiritual advisor was available who could make this possible and 'lead you into a good spiritual path.'

The Brahma Sukshma Naadi concluded with a list of puja that I could perform – some of which I could do myself and others could be delegated – which is not an ideal option as the puja I had learnt from my first encounters with the Naadi really require me to engage my own energy and dedication. Last in the suggested puja it says: "Best if he himself undertakes a pilgrimage to certain spiritual spots and holy places. He himself will know where to go."

The Stars Point the Way

It was true: I did know where to go. There were the temples from the first reading, which I would have loved to visit to do the suggested puja but, at that time, it would have been impossible. Could this be my call to India? Right now?

Kim told me that once I had made the above consultations from the leaves I could now ask the Naadi five specific questions. This part is called the Arundra Kandam and will give specific answers to personal questions. Some of the questions I asked it were personal so I won't be sharing these but I did ask about going to India, about my work with television and also 'When will Sai Baba return?'

The oracle told me to go to India in about two months' time after the 16th January 2016 when the stars are in a perfect alignment for me and that my spiritual advisor (Kim I presume) will guide me about what to do. And, while there, "You will possess a great chance to go to the holy place Arunachala where Maharishi lived and there get the blessings of Maharishi himself and with this you will be helped to overcome all your obstacles and worries on your path."

The pilgrimage, it said, would also open the door to the television work I had been working towards. "You can do it. This is sure. But of now the karmic effect is still these causing obstacles and breaks for you to do it. But after following my advice as already told you accordingly in the palm leaf reading, then for sure you can do this TV show. And this will give you the success you yearn for. And you will be happy by this event."

I'm sure some reading this will also be interested to know when Sathya Sai Baba will return but the oracle did not simply give a date. It said: "After minimizing your karmic effect you, yourself, will feel/see/understand about this event directly. You will possess a chance to see him through/in a vision in your dreams. The golden key to it lies in overcoming past karmic effect and you are already in the process of performing parts of the suggested parihams/remedies but yet it is not perfect but you have already been informed about this. With this you may have my blessings."

CHAPTER 4

ॐ

Mystic Journey to India

In January 2016 Kim Paisol suggested that he could arrange for me to visit India to do my remedies and travel with the astrologers who translated my Brahma Sukshma Naadi. The astrologer Mr. Prakash and his translator Gopie would take me to the temples and other locations to do the remedies that had been shown in all my Naadi readings to date. I could clear the karma in one sweep.

So much for my fretting about Indian roads and finding my way; now I would not only be able to visit all the places I wanted but I'd also have the Naadi astrologers with me who, I hoped, may answer my burning questions about the secrets of the Naadi. This would be the journey of a lifetime and something that I'm sure would radically change me spiritually and have far reaching implications for my fate. And it had all just dropped on my lap. Kim arranged everything and planned the itinerary, the hotels and hostels, and plotted a journey across Southern India so that I could visit the holy places prescribed in my Naadi leaves. According to my astrological chart, and from predictions in the leaves, an important period was ahead and it was highly auspicious if I went in February. Kim put it all together for free and I would pay Mr. Prakash and Gopie their expenses for the travel and temples charges and an optional fee for their time.

I would be going in just over four weeks. My only regret was that I would have loved to film it, as this would make an incredible documentary. Some years previously, Jane and I had proposed making a program about seeking out the Naadi readers to a number of TV channels and production companies but everyone I approached just couldn't understand the concept. It's a hard enough idea for professional psychics and mediums to understand so it stood no chance under the cold scrutiny of journalistically trained documentary makers or lobotomized reality TV makers. It would be fruitless to approach my old contacts, as I knew that nobody would make a quick decision or fund it in such a short time. I'd read that *Around The World In 80 Days*, which Michael Palin made way back in 1989 with the BBC, cost one million pounds to make, yet we planned to do much the same thing with nothing.

Let's Make a Movie

A few months before I decided to go to India, I had been talking to an independent filmmaker, Louis Frost, who makes his films on zero budgets. He was achieving great things on ridiculously low budgets but had turned his back on lucrative offers that would have compromised his creative goals. He would rather starve than make commercials or trash TV but he is such a charismatic person and has such great talent and original ideas that people will work for him for nothing just to get a good footage in their portfolio. I gave him a call and Louis jumped on the idea.

"Craig, this is great," enthused Louis. "I'll contact everyone I know and post a message on my Facebook pages to see if I can find a cameraman. It will be a tough call to find someone who can handle both camera and sound and be available to travel to India at such short notice. I'll get started on the release forms, running order and the rest today."

It's incredible how quickly Louis gets things together. In no time he's found a few potential candidates and he settled on Simon Knight, whom we arranged to meet at the elegant Pump House Restaurant that overlooks the Roman Baths hot spring in Bath. We agreed I would pay his flights, transport and hotels and, in return, he would film it for us and get a share of the net profits if we sell it. Meanwhile, Louis frantically put a plan together about how it should be filmed and gave me instructions of what he requires, shot sequences and notes about the style of presentation he envisioned and a formula to follow to ensure that every sequence had a good beginning, middle and end.

Three of us were going to make an international travelogue that would normally require a huge team and a massive budget. On the plus side we had a lot of talent and enthusiasm and a top of the range cinematic camera that is usually used for big screen movies. Louis had directed a number of feature films and had all the editing skills and knowledge to make this happen and we planned to upload for him the footage at every opportunity in India so that he could direct, check and edit everything from the UK.

Simon had been a BBC cameraman, and had traveled to third world countries when he'd worked as an air steward for British Airways, so was not going to panic if things went wrong. As well as being a good travel companion and a brilliant cinematographer, Simon also had another skill that would clearly be indispensable: at the start of his career with the BBC he was the man in the costume for the character Mr. Blobby on Noel's House Party. Now, for U.S. readers who have never heard of Mr. Blobby, he is a bulbous pink figure covered with yellow spots who has a permanently toothy grin and jiggling eyes. Mr. Blobby communicates only by saying the word "blobby" in a weird electronically distorted voice. The voice changes and gets faster or goes into a high squeaky tone depending on his mood.

"Sometimes I used to take my life in my hands doing the Blobby stuff," explained Simon. "They'd have me in the massive pink suit sweating away as Mr. Blobby hung out of helicopters. Sometimes I even wore a frogman suit under the costume so that I could suddenly emerge unexpectedly from swimming pools." In his 'Gotcha' segments Mr. Blobby would do pranks and barge, squealing, onto the set and knock everyone over in hilarious stunts. "You don't need to worry about me Craig," he joked "I've been used to some pretty surreal moments in my career so India will be no problem!"

So this was the man who was going to help me to get into the Indian temples and film it all? A ridiculous title for the show flashed across my mind: *Storming Heaven with Mr. Blobby* – this incongruous spiritual predicament is what the Hindus might call a leela, a Sanskrit word for the divine play: God's cosmic joke! God was clearly at work. He's sent me a top notch cameraman with a lot of guts and a great sense of humor!

A Pain in the Butt

I now have to interrupt the flow of the story to mention my not-so-funny hemorrhoids. Six months before planning all of the above I'd been to Harley Street in London and spent £4,000 to have them fixed using a non-invasive treatment that basically entailed putting electrodes up my bottom and zapping the piles till they shrank. Jane thought I was seeing a woman wearing kinky boots and a leather maid's outfit but the woman putting buzzing probes up my rectum was properly qualified. Jane insisted on accompanying me to London and waiting for me in nearby Oxford Street. "Poor me" says Jane as I limped to the café to meet her, "Having to get a complimentary cake and coffee at John Lewis with my loyalty card, while you pay someone a fortune to stick probes up your anus."

I should have spent the money on treating Jane, as, apart from having my hair standing on end, the electric hemorrhoid treatments didn't work and I was now painting the toilet bowl red every time I went to the loo. Despite doing yoga every day I was getting very, very tired until eventually I gave in and went to see the doctor for a blood test. I could hardly stand, hardly breathe and was seeing flashing lights. I had severe anemia and they rushed me to hospital for an emergency blood transfusion. The doctors couldn't understand how I was conscious with such a low red blood cell count – but they hadn't practiced yoga all of their lives.

It was a tough call as I am a total coward when it comes to blood and will faint at the sight of it. To make matters worse, during the week I was hospitalized, my daughter Danielle had her second baby (Damian) by cesarean section – no big deal that of course – and there were complications for her and the baby. I'd have loved to have been in the other hospital celebrating the birth rather than stuck in mine with a horrible bag of blood beside me. Being in hospital was frustrating and brings it home to you how short and precious our lives are. It made me all the more determined to go to India and fulfil my destiny.

When I looked back at some of my earlier Naadi readings they appeared to have foreseen these events and talked about how I would be unable to travel at this time as I'd be so tired but it would be okay after 16th January 2016 – the date just before I left hospital. The Naadi had seen my problem, though I think I would have used stronger words than 'tired' if I'd been the Maharishi making the forecast, and it had also seen my journey to India.

Naturally everyone I knew urged me not to go to rural India after all these problems but I felt that, if the Naadi could get it right about my illness, then it would also get it right about my predicted recovery. Mr. Prakash consulted his astrological almanac and made me re-book the flight and hotel to suit the auspicious signs he'd seen in my horoscope. Once the planets and stars were in the right position, I packed my rucksack, kissed my perplexed wife Jane goodbye and headed for Heathrow to meet Simon and head for India. We were given the best seats.

As the aircraft engines hummed, I drifted towards sleep and dreamed about both of my grandfathers – one an explorer and the other a sailor – who were there urging me on and encouraging me to embrace the day. "A great adventure is ahead Craig," I heard the spirit say. As I drifted in and out of sleep I recalled their stories of adventure that they shared with me as a boy.

CHAPTER 5

ॐ

Spirit of Adventure

My primary purpose for being in India was to do the karmic remedies prescribed by the Naadi oracle, in order to clear my spiritual path and negate the effects of past life karma, but now there was the huge challenge of filming it all, too. With a crew of one, plus Louis back in the UK directing and editing by phone, email and Skype, this was clearly going to be a monumental task. Our intention was to make a top-quality program suitable for broadcast on a high quality TV channel such as Discovery, National Geographic or BBC 2. Simon and I carried a comparatively heavy camera and sound kit. We would rely on the RED for the cinematic and static shots and a small, lightweight camera for live action, unexpected moments and reactions. We, of course, had no crew or researchers to run ahead of us, plan the itinerary or set up locations; we were simply going to roll with events as they unfolded and, hopefully, capture everything we could on camera.

On one level it was an impossible way to shoot a program but the suddenness of it all gave us the freedom to film a real-life adventure as it naturally unfolds. During the filming, and throughout the editing and post-production, we all had a sense that a hidden force was directing us from afar. Everyone who became involved later during the production and promotion also had an eerie feeling that they were being guided by divine providence.

Jane did not want to make the arduous journey to India and had her doubts about my health as well our frantically organized plans. This could be a dangerous and uncertain time. She'd accompanied me to India in the past to see Sathya Sai Baba in Puttaparthi, near Bangalore, so she knew what rural India is like and had managed very well, despite a few freaky moments. But this journey was different;

this was a 'bloke thing'. Jane had also not consulted her leaves, and, although she was just as stunned as I was by its insights, she did not want to consult it. She felt that her spirit guides had already revealed her past life through her intuition but, unlike me, she did not feel the need to get confirmation of her insights.

Jane was, nevertheless, supportive of my mad plans but, in return for all this altruistic goodwill and letting me off the leash and so on, I was to return with quarry.

"You can go to India but I expect you to bring me Indian treasures," she joked. "I see a big, sparkly ruby ring coming to me – of this I am certain. Make sure you fulfil this prophecy". The money I was spending on the trip could have bought us both a vacation somewhere nice so I guess she struck a fair bargain.

Spiritual Non-conformist

I find it hard to live as required by normal society. It amazes me how most people sleepwalk through life and never stop to marvel at the impossibility of simply being here or ponder why a tiny blue dot in the vastness of black infinite space should sustain this strange theatre of the human story. The conformist, mind-numbing banality of most people's lives betrays these billions of years of fiery creation and the brutal path of evolution that has brought us to this point in time. Everywhere the banal triumphs: mindless television dribbles the same lazy, greedy messages into our homes and we suck it all in. Today we can have it all but we miss the very reason we came here in the first place and few people are prepared to take a chance or embark on risky adventures.

The desire to seek out adventure has been instilled in me through the family stories told to me as a child by my grandfathers whom I'd dreamt about on the plane journey. My grandfather Frank Devonshire – on my mother's side of the family – joined up for the First World War at the age of 14 but one of the sergeants realized he was underage and, instead of marching him to the trenches, had him reassigned to the Ordnance Corps. At that time, my granddad was fiercely patriotic and told me that all he wanted to do was 'kill Germans', but instead he was shipped off to Africa as cartographer. He was furious at his exclusion from the front but clearly, through this twist of fate, his life was saved. They shipped him to colonial

Nigeria, gave him a white horse, a theodolite, a gun and supplies carried by a small rebellious team of Yoruba speaking tribesmen. His instructions were to map the last unexplored areas of Nigeria for the British army.

When I was a child of 5, Grandad told me many enthralling true stories of his time in Nigeria, many of which would now be considered inappropriate to tell a young child. Marked on my memory are his tales of how he had to shoot his white horse named 'Surley'. The mare had sleeping sickness and he said that shooting her through the head was one of the hardest things he'd ever had to do. Without her he felt isolated and alone in the wilderness. He was also more vulnerable and, on one occasion, had to control the tribesmen under his command by firing his gun and lashing out with his whip as they tried to steal the payroll safe.

They called him 'the little man with the big temper' and, like many British colonialists, he ruled by fear. He was the only one of the cartographers to make it back intact. After the three-year expedition, some had died of tropical diseases, some became alcoholics, some were killed by the natives and the remaining two both shot themselves in the head. Granddad was sent out to look for one of his fellow cartographers who'd gone missing and found his charred body atop a mountain by one of the trig points. The coins that had been in the man's pocket were melted and fused together as a block, which suggested to my granddad, and the inquest that followed, that he'd been struck by lightning.

My fertile young mind soaked up his incredible stories that were reminiscent of the adventures of Haggard's protagonist Allan Quatermain from *King Solomon's Mines*. He told about how he walked into a village of cannibals who were terrified of him because of his white skin, how he set up a trig point on forbidden mountain despite everyone's protests and was considered a hero for taking on the Vodun (voodoo) spirits and how he coped with medical crises, dangerous animals, snake bites and so on in the middle of nowhere.

Sinking of the Rohilla

Meanwhile, back in England, my other grandfather – Ernest Parker – at the age of 14, had run away to sea with his brother Ben. They were cabin boys aboard the WW1 hospital ship, the SS Rohilla, that was bringing wounded soldiers back from the trenches and struck the rocks at Saltwick Nab near Whitby, North Yorkshire, at 4 am 29 October 1914. The weather was so bad that the rescue crew could not get the lifeboats out when she floundered and the S.S. Rohilla had only 20 lifeboats herself, which was not enough to evacuate the passengers and crew. Eventually a rescue bid was made. It was the last ever rescue by rowing lifeboat and, despite the strenuous efforts of the lifeboat men, eighty four people perished. The Rohilla had been holed as it rammed the Scar. Her engines had been going full speed ahead and, within minutes, she filled with water and had lain broadside to the waves, breaking into three on the rocks.

Captain Neilson, the captain, was the first to save granddad's life. Five men had been already washed overboard from the Rohilla as they made for their lifeboat stations. Those on board the stricken ship knew it was going to be some time before a rescue bid could be made because the crashing waves and strong winds continued into the morning, frustrating all attempts to float the lifeboat from nearby Whitby. The rescue crew eventually had to lower the lifeboat down the other side of the cliff. By this time all but one of the Rohilla's own lifeboats had been washed away and time was running out. It took hours of toil for the seamen on the wrecked ship to position the lifeboat for launching and, by this time, 60 men were missing. The ship was breaking up, the funnel crashing down onto the boat deck, just missing the bridge where most of the one hundred and sixty nine survivors were clinging on. One of these survivors had been aboard the Titanic when it sank and said that the ordeal on the Rohilla was a far more terrifying experience.

Captain Neilson was kinder to his cabin boys than the cannibalistic Captain Dudley who ate my grandfather's uncle in 1848 in the story predicted by Edgar Allan Poe that I spoke about in one of my other books. Neilson shared out the contents of his wardrobe, draped one of his ornate coats around granddad, and tied him to the ship's railings. Despite the considerable distress the men were experiencing they all laughed at the boy lashed to the rails in the incongruous full dress uniform of a captain of the British India Line.

My grandfather was one of the last to be rescued in the heroic attempt by the lifeboat men, who rowed against the strong winds and currents. He was very lucky because one of the lifeboats reached him just before the Rohilla was smashed to pieces against the sharp rocks.

The young man who pulled him from the water comforted him in his shock and fear.

"Ben, Ben, where's Ben?" cried granddad through his tears. He then blacked out and later woke up in hospital. When he had recovered he was taken to the mortuary to try to identify the body of his brother among the others, but he could not be found. He was eventually discovered to be alive in another hospital and the two brothers would share and remember their fearsome experience for the rest of their lives.

Many years later my granddad and Nan were on vacation in Yorkshire when they decided to visit Whitby for the first time since granddad had been a boy. Their first stop was to look for the old lifeboat station and, to their surprise and delight, not only was it still standing, but part of it had been turned into a museum. The wreck of 'The Rohilla' took prominent place amongst the proud history of the Whitby lifeboat men. There were pieces of the wreckage, telegrams informing relatives about the disaster, photographs, and a large model of 'The Rohilla' herself. Nan and granddad stood and admired the model.

An old man in a duffel coat came over to them. "Are you interested in 'The Rohilla'?" he said.

"Very much so," replied granddad.

"I have a personal experience of that dreadful day," the man continued "I was one of the lifeboat men who went out that night. I remember pulling aboard a young cabin boy. He was tied to some wreckage and was crying for his brother." This stranger in a duffel coat was the very lifeboat man who, forty years earlier, had saved granddad's life and who was now working in the museum. Now, remarkably, their paths had crossed again.

They say that life turns on a sixpence. In these old wartime stories we are reminded of how slim the odds are that we are here on earth in this current form. We are the product of the survivors. If my granddad Devonshire had not been prevented from going to the trenches and instead sent to Africa, my mother would not have been born. If my granddad Parker had not been lashed to the railings and saved, my father would never have been. My father, too, was intrigued by the twists and turns of fate that appear sometimes to contort to bring our life to existence. In the Second World War he was training to be a bomber pilot and was being prepared to be in the first wave of the planes that would bomb the beaches of the Japan invasion. He knew that none of the pilots would survive the attack as they would be the first to go in. Throughout his life said that he owed his life to the dropping of the A Bomb on Hiroshima: he died on August 6.

No matter how many times you may visit India, it is always a culture shock and, no matter how much sleep you get on the journey from the UK, there's always a lot of jetlag. India is a bombardment to the senses. As we drove from the airport, strange scenes, faces, smells and sounds crashed towards us as the taxi drove at break-neck speed, near-missing everything by a fraction of an inch. The broken roads are frantic with babies and families being carried on single mopeds, people hanging precariously onto buses and rusty Leyland lorries, overloaded bicycles wobble through fast traffic while demented bus drivers stop for no one except the cows that nonchalantly munch their way across the freeway as vehicles fly around them.

We were staying at a beach resort just outside of Chennai (Madras). It was a beautiful tropical resort with tidy green lawns flicked by water and rows of palm trees interspaced by white statues of Indian gods and elephants. We had four days booked here, which would give Simon and me enough time to recover, prepare ourselves for time ahead and do some initial filming. We needed to make sure all the equipment was working and the quiet hotel setting was the perfect place to take some shots of me talking to camera. There was a lot of preparatory filming to do and, even though we had no idea what was ahead of us, we, nonetheless, needed to establish the story and explain to the viewer why I was in India.

Two of us were doing what would normally take months of planning by a substantial team. It would have been a hard task even with a full support crew and research team but we were determined to make something fantastic to the highest spec. that would inspire people and that I could sell through my contacts in America. With no money and no crew we set about making a movie that was good enough to compete at the Cannes Film Festival.

CHAPTER 6

ॐ

Tuning in to India

I had arranged with Santosh Acharya, who was the translator for the Naadi reader Mr Sivasakthi, to meet me at my hotel near Chennai and deliver me the metal plate that had been made as part of the Naadi remedies that he had done on my behalf. We filmed this as part of the TV program but the sound and lighting were poor so most of it had to be dropped in the edit. However Santosh told me some interesting things about the Naadi leaves so I now include a transcript of the interview below.

Craig: You did my Naadi reading just from my thumbprint and you and the Naadi reader knew nothing about me. We both knew Vivek but all you had to go with was my thumbprint. So how, with just a thumbprint, can you find the correct leaves?

Santosh: The thumbprint just helps us to find the bundle, which may contain your prediction and your exact leaf.

Craig: And finding the exact leaf from the bundle involves you asking me strange questions such as 'Am I involved in mining?' and all sorts of strange things?

Santosh: Yes, we just read out what is on the leaf and all you need to do is confirm if what is said is right or not.

Craig: I was amazed when, after a series of rejected leaves, you read on the leaf that my ex-wife's name was Tina. Nobody could know that as I have never published this fact in my books or anything like that. All written on an ancient leaf; amazing. How old are the leaves?

Santosh: More than one thousand years.

Craig: You say you read only what's written on the leaf but sometimes astrology is mentioned too. When you make an astrological reference is this also written on the leaf?

Santosh: We only read what is in the leaf but if there are some doubts we can clarify things using astrology.

(Santosh and this Naadi reader were only ever given my thumbprint and I did not tell them anything at all about me. They told me my time and date of birth – which they read from the leaves. You can identify a fake Naadi astrologer if he asks your date of birth. With your DOB one can cast a horoscope and use this for the reading but a true Naadi astrologer will work only from your thumb impression. After taking out the leaves, a Naadi reader might ask you one or two yes-or-no questions to confirm that the leaf is yours. If your answers are 'no', they go to other leaves.)

Craig: After mentioning my ex-wife's name, the leaf went on to give my mother's name, my father's name and my siblings. It said that I was born in hospital and then gave an exact description of all the important facts about my life to date. Does everyone get this same level of information – even when they come from places with languages such as Chinese or Korean?

Santosh: Yes people from all over the world get similar information.

(Skeptics insist that people with a credulous disposition visit Naadi readers and so are easily duped into giving away information about themselves and family names. They claim Naadi readers eavesdrop on clients in their waiting rooms and use cold reading techniques to extract and feed-back information. It is alleged that most of the information is provided by the client from their reactions to yes or no questions and from subconscious body signals. This may be the case with fake readers but as I explained in my first book on the Naadis I went to great lengths to ensure that Santosh and the other readers could glean no information whatsoever about me. I used a friend as a proxy to make the arrangements and I used a fake email account and Skype address. When talking to a Naadi reader it is important never to give your date of birth and do not try to give him information: only say yes or no.)

Craig: It's incredible that Agastya Muni and the other maharishis/siddhas who wrote these leaves could comprehend strange names in different languages – they knew that my mother's name was Ethel for example – not a commonly heard name in India. How did they describe things that had not been invented such as cars, airplanes, televisions and computers?

Santosh: The name is given to the translator as it is already in the language.

(Santosh's answer was a little vague but I am told by other sources that an airplane is described as a machine that flies in the air, a television is a machine of sound and light and a train is called line of carts on wheels.)

Craig: So it was first written in Sanskrit?

Santosh: No not Sanskrit, ancient Tamil.

(The leaves were translated from Sanskrit into ancient Tamil. Carbon dating shows some of them to be about 400 years old but it is claimed that the leaves have been copied and re-copied over the centuries. Claims have been made in the Indian media that many fake leaves have been produced from an area called Vaitheeswaran Koil.)

Craig: You tell me about things that have already happened in my life from the leaves and then there's predictions. From your experience, do the predictions always come true or just sometimes? Can things change the prediction?

Santosh: If things are not done, the prediction may change.

Craig: So you are saying that if a person does the remedies it makes sure the better karma comes your way and better things happen to you. So if a person does the remedies do the predictions change and future readings from the leaves reflect this? Will the time of your death change for example? In other words, will the Naadi predictions change as you do more remedies?

Santosh: After telling about the remedies positive things that are predicted happen in your life without fail and the negativity falls away. Just getting your leaf is determined by good karma.

Craig: When I read the Indian press I see that there is talk of many palm leaf readers that cheat and make fake palm leaves and so on. Is there a lot of that going on?

Santosh: Yes I recognized my current Naadi reader and I am working with him but I would not go to anybody else. He knows the astrology signs well and the palm leaves well and knows the exact meaning of the ancient Tamil and he never alters a single word. Even if it upsets the client he will not change it. Sometimes the leaves say there are unpleasant things coming.

(Santosh told me later that when he first worked as a translator for another Naadi reader the reader cheated. He would, for example give the same typed reading to different people and alter the names to fit. When Santosh discovered what was going on he quit his job but was fortunate to meet this sincere reader.)

Craig: Clearly many people have come to you for readings. Of all the cases, what are some of the remarkable things that have happened such as what predictions have happened and how quickly?

Santosh: One lady was given three months to live and was told the two days over which she would pass away. She had cancer but her brother, husband and son did not know about it. If she lives after this date you can bring her and we can read another Naadi leaf.

Craig: So the leaf is saying she may die but if she passes that date she will continue and there's another leaf for her. So if she did remedies she could extend her life?

Santosh: Yes.

Craig: My leaf tells me when I'm going to die, pretty much to the date, and I was okay with that.

Santosh: Not everyone tolerates this and these facts so many of the readers change this.

Craig: So they want the reading to sound good but this is not what the maharishis that wrote this wanted. Tell me, who are these maharishis? I know that in Hinduism mythology they talk about the great founding rishis called the 'Sapta Rishis'

(The recording here was poor so I have not been able transcribe what Santosh said. The traditional view is that the Naadis were transcribed by Agastya who is one of the ancient Saptarshis, a revered Vedic saint. Agastya is also the Indian astronomical name of the star of Canopus and is said to be the 'cleanser of waters', since its rising coincides with the calming of the waters of the Indian Ocean. He was son of Pulasthya, son of Brahma. Agathiyar is the first Siddhar yogi. Siddhar were spiritual adepts who possessed the ashta siddhis, or the eight supernatural powers. A reference to Maharishi Agastya is made in Paramahansa Yogananda's Autobiography of a Yogi, Chapter 33: "Babaji, Yogi-Christ of Modern India", p. 333, in the statement "A considerable poetic literature in Tamil has grown up around Sage Agastya, a South Indian avatar. He worked many miracles during the centuries preceding and following the Christian era, and is credited with retaining his physical form even to this day." Later in my journey I touch the feet of a living Siddhar yogi who, is it is claimed, will live for 200 years and can sleep in a raging fire.)

Santosh: .... Some of them work using astrology who have written the Naadi predictions in the palm leaves. Some of them have written very long predictions and some leaves are very simple.

Craig: I've noticed the difference when I've consulted different Naadi readers. Something that interests me personally, as I work with a different form of prediction with my work as a psychic medium, and in the Naadi leaf reading you gave to me it said that I would make predictions about things such as predicting gas clouds that will affect the world. I feel the Naadi may have information not just for us as individuals but for all of mankind. There may be messages to help us avoid calamity. Perhaps we can change it.

Santosh: Yes by group meditation. Everything that is outside us, is inside us also.

Craig: You can ask the Naadi questions such as 'will I be a rich man?' and so on but I believe the Naadi's real purpose is as a guide to self-realization. It is a mirror into the One. I find with my own work as a medium, if the person comes with spiritual intent and asks for spiritual guidance then the accuracy of the spirit evidence increases. The more spiritual the question, the more powerful and accurate comes the answer. Is it the same for the Naadi?

Santosh: Yes.

Craig: Most Western people will find all this impossible and will say it's all just looked up on the Internet or that you ask leading questions and you reply with things the person wants to hear but it's been proven to me though these readings that no way is this the case. You knew nothing about me before the reading and I gave you no clues to find out things. It's absolutely astonishing.

Since I had the consultation with you I have consulted some more Naadis, such as the Brahma Naadi, and I notice that the past lives are similar in theme but different in detail. Does it mean that when the Naadi reveals a past life that they are different lives or different interpretations of the same life? All my past lives were in India. Are past lives always set in India or can they be interpreted as past lives in a different culture. Do the leaves reveal past lives in places like Rome or China?

Santosh: The name may be different. The name of China may be different for example. It may have been known by a different name at that time. Past lives can be from anywhere.

Craig: Just as the Naadi may reveal the future of the world, maybe it can reveal the lost history of the world too and tell of times and civilizations long forgotten. I would love to know the secrets of the first religion called the Sanatana Dharma. Maybe it can even tell us about Atlantis?

Anyway I believe you have brought me my talisman made after the chanting of many mantras and as part of the remedies. What does the talisman mean? And also, I was told about the Jiva Naadi that can answer live questions put to it – do you also have access to this oracle?

Santosh: The talisman is a remedy that protects you from negativities and solves the problems that are yet to come in your life. Mr Shivashankti does not use the Jiva Naadi but he uses something similar called the AAsi Kaandam. For this the person just comes to us and sits with us and the Naadi gives all the answers to the questions that are on the person's mind.

Some say that the AAsi Kaandam is a way by which the Siddhas communicate to their believers, followers and disciples and is a tool to spiritual realization. Some claim that the reading will appear on the leaf and then mysteriously erase itself once the reading is completed. Before any more is revealed the instructions given by the leaf must be followed to the very word – no matter how difficult or daunting they may be. It is a direct link to the Siddhas.

Santosh passed me the talisman in an envelope. It is a small square of silver with my protective Shiva mantra, written on it in Sanskrit, that was found in the palm leaf. Once the mantras had been chanted over a number of weeks the talisman was made in the ceremonial fires, taken out and then sprinkled with sacred Vibhuti ash. Santosh tells me to wear it at all times. It can be put into a pendant and worn at the level of the heart.

The Presence of the Past

The day after filming the interview with Santosh, I decided to get Jane the ruby ring I'd promised her and also a pendant for my new talisman. Soon we'd be driving to remote areas so I needed to sort things out before events overtook us.

Near to the hotel I found a small shop that not only sold lovely rings but also was a specialist in antiquarian and very old items. The shopkeeper – Omar Shah – was a very spiritual man and we got talking about Hindu philosophy and what I was planning to do in India – not the usual chit chat you'd expect to have with a shopkeeper. We were soon really enjoying one another's company and chatting as if we'd been friends for years. Without my saying anything about my career back home, out of the blue he mentioned that he sensed I had spiritual powers (siddhis) including the ability to see into the past and future. This was a strange thing to say to a stranger but it gave me an idea: I told him about my reason for being in India and my work at home as a medium so asked him if he would let me film something with him.

I would practice some psychometry on his collection of ancient artifacts to see if I could correctly read the history of the object and its previous owners. As well as making an interesting piece to camera, this would also be a fascinating experiment to use my spiritual gifts to 'tune in' to ancient India.

Psychometry with Ancient Artifacts

Psychometry is the psychic ability to discover facts about an event or person by touching inanimate objects associated with them. When I first developed my mediumistic abilities and now when I teach others to become mediums, psychometry is used a way to kick-start psychic abilities. A psychically sensitive person will get impressions of the memories that are held in the residual energy of the objects they are asked to hold. These 'memories' are impressed into the psychic's mind and experienced as images and feelings from which we can describe the character and life history of the object's previous owners. This technique is used in psychic development circles to teach new mediums how to initially connect with the inner impressions they get from an object but later to do the same with a living person and eventually with the spirit communicators.

Psychometry can be developed as a psychic skill in its own right and, in my own work, I have demonstrated it on the BBC where I correctly told the history of objects handed to me by museum curators. This gift can be used as part of a personal reading or for a specific task such as building a character profile from a murder weapon. It can also help you to attune to the history and energy of places and, in this case, to the holy vibrations of India.

The first object the collector handed me was a Buddha statue. I described the person he'd bought it from and correctly explained how this artifact originated from Tibet and had a prayer hidden inside in it to the goddess Tara. I gave similar readings for a number of very old objects from his collection. Some of these had been refused export licenses and were later to be donated to an Indian museum. Amongst them were a number of ancient Buddhist relics that had been smuggled out of Afghanistan by monks fleeing the war.

One of the most interesting was what he called a 'prava' though I cannot find the word on the internet or know if I have the right name here. This was a type of wand with three demons at the top that represent anger, jealousy and hatefulness. These were mounted on a staff made of crystals and gold with strange heads carved into it. At the base was a clear quartz crystal and a point made of gold. The juxtaposition of the gems and semi-precious stones corresponded to the five elements and the planets. The golden point of this object would be placed on the chakra points of an ill person to promote healing.

I opened my psychic perceptions as I held a number of these curious wands and, in each case, the energy that they contained nearly knocked me sideways. This was a shock to me as I had always been skeptical of the claims made by crystal healers and therapists. I had assumed that all the fuss made over crystals was simply New Age hocus-pocus, and maybe a bit of placebo effect thrown in, but here I felt something that physically shook my body and made me feel giddy for some time afterwards.

The final object that Omar Shah handed me was a Shiva Lingam stone of about 9 inches length. This is an elongated egg-like sacred stone that occurs naturally at the banks of the Narmada River in Onkareshwar, Mandhata, one of India's sacred holy sites. They are formed by a mineral called Cryptocrystalline Quartz which, legends say, were implanted in the riverbed by a meteorite millions of years ago. These stones are said to radiate a powerful vibration that will purify a temple or home. They are very rare and they are found once a year in the river when it is very low just before the monsoon season.

By now I was psychically very attuned and sensitive to vibration and as I took hold of the Shiva Lingam I was completely overwhelmed by its energy. I could feel my chakras – the spiritual energy centres in the spinal column – light up and my whole spiritual body felt that it was illuminated too. I described the owner as someone who lived in Kashmir and was a very holy man; he had given this lingam with special instruction and it was not to be sold in the normal way. In my mind's eye I could see the man stood with me.

Omar Shah then explained that I was right in what I said as the lingam had been owned by Pandit Vishnu Baclecinath who came from Tulmul in Kashmir. He is a holy man with many devotees and will spiritually heal people using a number of secret techniques. He is now a very elderly person.

The lingam was originally found near the Amarnath Cave, which is a Hindu shrine at Jammu in Kashmir and situated at a high altitude in the snowy mountains. It is considered as being one of the holiest shrines in Hinduism. Inside is a giant stalagmite, which is formed by freezing water drops and has formed into the shape of a Shiva lingam. The lingam grows and shrinks with the phases of the moon. This is the cave where Shiva explained the secret of life and eternity to his divine consort Parvati.

I had felt a deep bond with the lingam. I knew that none of these objects were for sale because of their antiquity; they were heading for the museums and could not be exported but I went back to visit Omar on my return to the airport and asked if he would sell it.

Omar said that he believed that this lingam was meant for me as the Pandit had given strict instructions about its sale and that Omar would know when the owner would be found. It is said that by destiny everyone has their own lingam as the signature of a person's soul is embedded in it and, if you are to own a lingam in this life, then it will find you. Omar said that he felt the lingam was for me and was prepared either to give it to me or let me take it with me back to the UK and pay for it when I got home or whenever I could afford it. Recently Indian law had changed and now lingams are available for export. From a spiritual perspective some Hindus consider that their distribution and energetic influence may help the desperate state of the planet.

Omar also said that he felt that one day I would be opening a spiritual centre and that the lingam would be the centrepiece of this holy place. This was no clever sales tactic – he was offering me the lingam at the price he paid for it, which was very low even by Indian standards. It was odd, too, as the early Naadi predictions had spoken about 'opening spiritual centres around the world'. I bought the lingam and also a beautiful ruby ring for Jane. While I was having adventures, she was home alone so deserved the best I could afford.

There is also something very strange about my Lingam stone that I have never heard of before: it has a liquid centre that you can feel and hear when it's shaken. Sometimes it gets noticeably hot or cold when it is held. The lingam also has an extraordinary energy about it that others feel as well. Some say they see a soothing golden light when they hold it. When I first showed it to Jane she, too, saw a holy man in her mind's eye and described a golden healing light coming from the stone.

I returned with my purchase to my hotel and was thumbing through my Naadi readings and for the present time was shocked to read: "The native has to keep a Shiva Lingam and worship it. Shiva Lingam is the symbolism of both male and female together." It looked as if some of the Naadi prophecies were coming true already and I'd only just started my mystic journey.

We had a few more days in the hotel before we were to meet the Naadi reader Mr. Prakash and his brother Gopie who would act as translator. They would be picking us up from the hotel and we'd be travelling around Southern India to perform the Naadi remedies I'd been prescribed.

At the hotel we filmed all footage needed of me talking to camera and explaining what the Naadi predictions are and why I'm in India to perform the remedies to clean my karma. Now we needed some general footage of street scenes and other filler shots that could be used to help link the activities, travels and various scenes together. It was either this or slither over and get some shots of the dismal looking *Chennai Snake Park*, horrifically built next to the *Children's Park*, which we'd passed the other day on the way to the hotel. It looked like a great family day out with its badly painted signs, rickety snake nests, petting area and writhing dens of vipers.

Instead of exploring these silly ideas we took a taxi to Mahabalipuram, the local village, to get some good general footage of me walking through streets, feeding a cow and interacting with local people. We turned a corner, crossed a lawn and, to our astonishment, realized that we were looking at one of India's most grandiose ancient sites. Towering all over the hills in front of us were the incredible Cave Temples of Mahabalipuram that overlook Coromandel Coast of the Bay of Bengal. I know that now but it was breathtaking to see unexpectedly something so magnificent.

As Simon frantically searched for a spare battery for the camera I looked for a guide to show us around. We had an idea: I would use my psychometry skills to see if I could work out the history of the place and we could get confirmation or disprove my insights.

Mysterious Mahabalipuram

Mahabalipuram are a series of eerie rock-hewn temples that sit atop a hill and overlook a spectacular view of the Bay of Bengal. What you first notice, as you enter the complex, is a precariously balanced rock that I found out later is called Krishna's Butterball. It's a gigantic granite boulder, of approximately 6 meters high and 5 meters wide and weight around 250 tons, that rests balanced on a short incline. It looks as if it will roll wildly downhill with the slightest touch but is said to have been resting at the same precarious spot for 1,200 years.

Krishna's Butterball looks like a 20 feet tall egg, balanced in a gravity-defying upright position, perched on an area of less than two square feet on the sloping, slippery hillside. Nobody really knows how it maintains its unbelievable balance on such a small spot for such a long time. The mysterious granite rock from some angles looks almost like a perfect sphere. Many people think of this rock as a natural formation but geologists tell us that there is no way that the rock could become this shape by erosion, flowing water or wind. It sits completely isolated on a small hill that is devoid of any other large rocks or boulders.

The question arises: who put it there if it is not a natural feature? Today we'd have trouble moving a 250 ton rock uphill even with the benefit of massive cranes and Lorries. How was it done 1,200 years ago without modern day technology?

The base of the rock is somehow magically 'glued' to the ground. In 1908, then-governor of the city of Madras, Arthur Havelock, made an attempt to use seven elephants in tandem to push the rock from its position but with no success. It is said that Pallava king Narasimhavarman, 630–668 AD, also made a failed attempt to move the boulder.

An elephant can push or pull 6 tons so the combined power of seven elephants is 42 tons but the Butterball didn't move an inch from its 2ft square base. Some question whether the rock was placed there by extra-terrestrials or by a people who had super human powers such as the people of the lost continent Kumar Kandam that I will talk about later in this book. How on earth did it get there and how does a 250 ton rock stand on a 2ft square base on a slope without tumbling down the hill? Krishna's Butterball is an impossibility but perhaps the original name of the rock holds a clue to its mysterious origin?

In 1969, a tour-guide is said to credit its present name, Krishna's Butterball, to Indira Gandhi who was on a tour of the city but the original name comes from the Tamil word Vaan Irai Kal, which, according to the Atlas Obscura, translates to "The Stone of Sky God" which, of course, fuels speculation about UFOs. Unlike most of the rock in the surrounding area, there are no carvings on Krishna's Butterball and carving was forbidden since the time of king Narasimhavarman. This suggests that the rock was there long before his reign from 630 AD so, to know its origins, we must look far back in time.

Psychometry at Mahabalipuram

Simon filmed Krishna's Butterball, and me exploring the remains of the upper temples while I interacted with the guide and gave my psychic insights as to what I felt was once there and why the temples were built. Psychic Archeology is a favorite of mine as I'd done a number of programs in the past with the BBC to see if my psychic insights matched the knowledge of museum curators and archeologists pitched against me.

After a short time in contemplation I was soon spiritually open and in the proper state of mind to do some psychometry on the structures. As I touched the ancient rocks to give my impressions to the guide, my head flooded with images of huge fires and the smell of smoke. I 'knew' that the main purpose of this place was for night worship and, under the indigo skies, the place would have come alive with torch light and huge crackling fires. I was particularly attracted to a large circular area that was carved out of the granite and, as I put my hands on it, 'saw' that this was the place where the most important ceremonies happened. For some reason, I felt that this easily overlooked area, carved into a huge stone bowl, was the key to the whole place. Our guide explained that here was the centre of the night ceremonies where huge fires were used to make massive vats of butter that would be poured over the stone images of the gods. Vast quantities of liquid butter were used, he said, that would today fill many, juggernauts.

As I touched the cold walls of the temples I seemed immediately to know all about its history as if I were being told it by the voice of the residual vibrations that had been left there centuries before. One thing I felt more than anything was that this place was far more ancient than the 1,500 years old that historians had claimed. The whole place had been carved out of solid granite so, in many ways, was hard to date and I found out later that dating the site is a hot topic with archeologists and that Mahabalipuram's origins are shrouded in mystery. I was getting feelings and half-memories of being far back in time, way before Stonehenge and the history we know.

The fact that we had stumbled into the temples, and that I knew absolutely nothing about them at the time, made my psychic insights all the more intriguing. What was it that I was seeing and why did I have this feeling I was standing somewhere far more ancient than what my guide was telling me. There was a sense, too, that we were only seeing a small part of the temple. The guide told us that there are other shore temples, on the coast below, which are also part of the Mahabalipuram group but I felt that, in centuries past, you could view the rest of the temple from this place stretching far away to the horizon. This was a focal point for others below, who would look up to this fiery mountain against the starry night sky.

It was only when I sat down to write and do my research for this book that I discovered that many of my odd insights could be right. In April 2002 the controversial historian Graham Hancock joined a team of divers from the Indian National Institute of Oceanography and the Scientific Exploration Society based in Dorset, UK, to survey the ocean bed near Mahabalipuram.

Graham Hancock has challenged orthodox history, in his books such as *'Underworld – Flooded Kingdoms of the Ice Age'*, that there was once a vanished early civilization, which was destroyed by a cataclysm such as a massive worldwide flood. When they dived he did not expect to have some of these theories confirmed but their survey revealed a vast undersea network of temples and the submerged ruins of the city. Afterwards he commented, "I have argued for many years that the world's flood myths deserve to be taken seriously, a view that most Western academics reject ... But here, in Mahabalipuram, we have proved the myths right and the academics wrong." Graham Hancock claims that the submerged ruins may date back to the last Ice Age when sea level was 100 meters lower. "Mahabalipuram, with its neglected legends of the Seven Pagodas and the flooded city of Bali, lies at 12.37 degrees north and would have been at least 50 kilometers from the sea at the Last Glacial Maximum." (The Last Glacial Maximum was at about 24,500 BCE. Is this what I was 'seeing' when I did my psychometry on the granite walls?)

Two years after his dives the tsunami of 2004 unearthed some of the treasures long hidden beneath the sea. As the tsunami receded, centuries old sand deposits were washed away revealing lost treasures, including granite sculptures, temple ruins, bronze statues and other manmade structures. The survey of Mahabalipuram continues and promises to reveal many more secrets of ancient days.

Before leaving I climbed into one of the areas carved out of the black granite rock where the guide told me that people in the past would chant the mantra Om. I took a deep breath and, in this dark grotto, chanted "Ommmmmm." The whole hillside felt as if it was resonating and reverberating with my bass mantra as my voice joined with the residual vibrations of the ancients who sat here thousands of years ago doing the same. Few places on earth have such a vibrant connection with times long gone.

As a final gesture, and to bless our way forward, I made a small offering at a nearby shrine to Ganesha that was manned by a solitary priest. Here I bought fruit as an offering and chanted "Om Gam Ganapataye Namaha" – a simple beej mantra that evokes the spirit of Ganesha, the elephant-headed boy who is the son of the god Shiva and goddess Parvathi. This mantra is traditionally chanted when starting a great journey so that obstacles on the path can easily be overcome.

As we as left we could see Krishna's Butterball still precariously balanced on its hillside, silhouetted against a fiery orange sky. We now had some fabulous footage for the program in the bag and felt that our pilgrimage had really started on an auspicious note. As we found our battered taxi I had a sense of mild melancholy thinking about these ancient ruins and the magnificent lost days of India's past. I was reminded of the same eerie feeling I'd had some years before as Jane and I watched the sun set over the Palatine Hill and the ruins of the Roman Forum. Mahabalipuram has a similar, slightly sad, sense of the past that here cast its shadow over the present. As the car set off again into the modern world's blight of dense, wild traffic, I relaxed, enjoying my revelry and wondering what other mysterious marvels lay ahead.

CHAPTER 7

ॐ

Ancient Thiruvannamali

The psychometry experiments at the shop and at Mahabalipuram had gradually opened my aura to the vibrations of everything around me. Psychics and mediums know that it is wise to keep your psychic sensitivities closed in daily life. The aura is naturally protected from the intrusive thoughts and energies of the environment so that the medium is not drained and exhausted by the influences around him. When you 'open up' to demonstrate mediumship, techniques are used to expand the aura and allow it, temporarily, to become super-sensitive. These techniques allow the medium to be aware of the thoughts of people they meet, connect to the thoughts of the people in the spirit world and tune in to the energies in the environment and objects.

In normal life, it is spiritual suicide to allow the aura to remain open continuously because the medium's sensitivity becomes over enhanced, leaving them super-sensitive but also vulnerable to incoming negative vibrations. If they encounter someone with ill-will towards them, in an angry state of mind or a disturbed person with mental illness, then all these thoughts and vibrations can sweep through the aura and, if retained, can cause depression, anxiety and physical illness. Those who have trained their mediumship know how to switch it off when they are not using it for giving a reading or demonstration.

In normal circumstances, I would always keep my spiritual sensitivities wrapped up and my auric field functioning at a normal vibration. Sometimes, however, it is necessary to open the sensitivity for an extended period if there is a lot of spiritual work to be done. For example, when Jane and I made the TV series 'Our Psychic Family' we had to shoot six shows in two weeks, which meant filming back to back ghost hunts, celebrity readings and theatre demonstrations of mediumship with no time to rest or tune-out. Our psychic gifts were switched on and stayed on throughout the whole two weeks of intensive filming. We were shattered of course but, in our normal lives, we would not work with such spiritual intensity or we'd soon be very ill. It is a long-standing but unproven belief amongst spiritualists that badly managed mediumship can cause diabetes.

India was one of those exceptional times in which I allowed my aura and spiritual sensitivity to remain in overdrive for long periods. At Mahabalipuram I had been able to connect in ways that would not be possible if I remained in my normal daily awareness. Ahead of me I was to visit Mount Arunachala, one of the most sacred places in India, so I not only left myself spiritually open, but spent as much time as I could in meditation and doing a form of Spinal Breathing called Kriya yoga – a spinal energizing practice that uses the breath to drive energy up and down the spine.

By the time we were ready to set off on the adventures to do the Naadi remedies I was beginning to feel changes within me and was becoming super-sensitive to the vibrations of India. Simon, had noticed changes in himself as well. Everyday problems were less of a worry as we entered a state of mind that lifted us from our normal perspective so that we were seeing the bigger picture of our lives. It was like being on a mountain and looking down at ourselves, which is something many people feel when they connect with the spirit of India and something we were soon to do, literally, by climbing India's most sacred mountain.

We meet the Naadi Reader

This was my first meeting with the Naadi reader Mr Prakash and his brother and translator Gopinath. They had read and translated my Naadi leaves via my Danish friend Kim Paisol whom I wrote about earlier. Kim had arranged for them to take me to do the remedies prescribed in the leaves as well as the remaining remedies that I wrote about in my first book *Messages from the Universe*. He would also consult the leaves, when required, for further clarifications as we set out on our mystic journey.

I liked them immediately. Mr. Prakash radiated kindness, and Gopie, I could see, was a loyal and friendly soul. I knew immediately that these two were to become very important people in my life and there was a feeling – and I believe it was mutual – that we had a deep spiritual connection that may even have come from previous incarnations together. We were with good people; people we were meant to be with.

Pictured: Gopie, Craig and Mr. Prakash

The only problem was the language barrier. Mr. Prakash could speak some English and Gopie could speak and write English but their Indian accents were so strong that Simon and I usually totally misunderstood what was being said. We never knew if we were to get up at 3:00 am or meet at 3:00 pm, whether we were going down the road to buy an ice cream or about to travel for three days through the night. "Did he just say we are about to do a parachute jump?" Invariably what we thought we were about to do, turned out to be something completely different to what we expected. The uncertainty of everything was hilarious.

But we knew the plan for this first journey: we were heading for the town of Thiruvannamalai to walk up the holy mountain of

Arunachala. I dozed restlessly in the front seat of the car as we hurtled on broken roads through the dense Indian traffic and dreamed about Shiva and the adventures ahead. In a half-sleep revelry I mused how the Naadi leaves had predicted that I would take this journey to Shiva's mountain on this very date and then also to visit the ashram of Ramana Maharshi – the same prophecies that had been given by the satguru Sharavana Baba whom my wife, Jane, and I had met in London some months before my departure. It had all been predicted but it also felt out of place with my life back in England. I love to immerse myself in Indian teachings but may resist my attempts to show the closeness of Eastern and Western ideas.

Working as a Spiritualist medium I have often antagonized opinionated people when I talk about how Vedic teachings have parallels with many aspects of Spiritualist philosophy. The topic of reincarnation in particular irritates people when I mention it. The official Spiritualist line is that it is not to be included in a medium's address given from a Spiritualist podium but can be discussed at unofficial gatherings. Theosophy and the Spiritism of Allan Kardec have embraced reincarnation from the start but there's been fierce resistance within the UK's Spiritualist National Union churches. Talking about Shiva, Siddha yogis and 'magic mountains' gets you into even deeper water.

Shiva vs Spiritualism

Spiritualism is not a Christian religion. It is considered to be a 'universal religion' that is relevant to all faiths. The snag is that, despite this claim, many Spiritualists have hailed from a Christian background and draw heavily on the Christian faith and, even though the symbol for Spiritualism is a seven pointed star, they nonetheless insist on also putting up the cross above the church rostrum. This puzzled me when I first started working as a young medium for I'd read the work of the early pioneers such as Arthur Findlay and the debates between the first spiritualists and Cosmo Lang, the then archbishop of Canterbury, and it was clear to me that Spiritualism was a non-Christian religion but did not contradict the Christian message. At one of my first church services I quoted a passage by the Dalai Lama and was given a severe dressing down afterwards: "We'll not have any of that silly Buddha nonsense here!" said the church president who, I noticed, was wearing a rather large silver cross.

To know that I chant mantras to Shiva would probably alarm many Spiritualists who hold to the idea of a Creator God and refuse to look further. They can be just as bigoted as the materialist who believes that this universe is the result of a Big Bang that happened some fifteen million years ago that is expanding into galaxies and will eventually dissipate into a state of cold stillness and disintegration. In this model of the universe consciousness, the soul and the spirit hold no significance. When we are dead, awareness is gone and when the universe dies the incredible story of the all that has been dies with it. It is no more. Forever. (Assuming that 'forever' can take place without the existence of a material Universe to sustain time.) I can't buy into either model of the Universe.

In Hindu cosmology the universe is continually created and destroyed over vast periods of time like a heartbeat or breath that comes in and out of existence. In many ways this idea corresponds with contemporary science by suggesting that the Big Bang is not the beginning of everything, but is just the start of a present cycle preceded by an infinite number of universes and to be followed by another infinite number of universes. Once the Universe has been destroyed by Shiva, Brahma starts the creation once again. This creation-destruction cycle repeats itself endlessly. The process of becoming and ending goes on forever.

The Secrets of Shiva

Soon my journey will take me to ancient Shiva temples and holy sites where I am to begin the process of clearing my karma from the past lives described in my Naadi leaves. The god Shiva, and rituals made in his temples, will be central to all that happens on our journey. The fundamentalist Christian will think me damned and the materialist will say I'm deluded so let's pause for a moment and get to know what we mean by Shiva and his relevance to the Rishis who wrote the Naadis.

Shiva the god appears in the form the 'destroyer and transformer' within the Trimurti, which is the Hindu trinity that also includes Brahma and Vishnu. Shiva is the oblivion from which everything is born and eventually also returns. Shiva is the all prevailing darkness that is the backdrop to the light but, on another level, 'Shiva,' refers to the first yogi and guru called the Adiyogi or Adi Guru who appeared 15,000 years ago, on the banks of Kanti Sarovar, a glacial lake a few miles beyond Kedarnath in the upper regions of the Himalayas. Just as Jesus probably did not have blond hair and blue eyes, Shiva probably didn't have blue skin, though Kanti Sarovar is a very cold place and his body must have been coloured by the cold. The blue skin we see in the pictures of Shiva were probably the inventions of the artists who illustrated the stories centuries later.

The story goes that a crowd gathered around this strange looking man who sat motionless in meditation for months on end. They waited and waited but nothing happened. Eventually the miracle-seeking crowd became uninterested and there remained just seven people who followed the guru, wherever he went for 84 years, hoping that he would eventually give them some attention. Then on a full moon day – which is today celebrated as Guru Purnima – Shiva spoke and shared his knowledge of consciousness and the unlimited potential of being human with these seven dedicated men, who were to become known as the Saptarishis or Seven Sages and were to become the great teachers that took Shiva's teachings to the world.

Shiva, the man, may have been a fully realized being whose consciousness was fixed into the infinite void but who was to become a divine symbol for higher consciousness itself. The word 'Shiva' means literally, 'that which is not' which some take to mean that he represents that which is beyond the physical. Some describe it as 'nothingness' for only nothingness can contain everything. It is the darkness of the void that contains the light and allows it to shine.

From a religious perspective, Shiva is the third god in the Hindu triumvirate. The triumvirate consists of three gods who are responsible for the creation, upkeep and destruction of the world. The other two gods are Brahma and Vishnu. Brahma is the creator of the universe while Vishnu is the preserver of it. But the symbolism goes far deeper than this as these gods describe the fabric of all things and also our own make-up. Sathya Sai Baba – who, you will remember from my other book, triggered my journey – described Shiva with great clarity:

"Who is Shiva?" Divine Consciousness which pervades all living beings is none other than Shiva. This Divine Consciousness permeates not only human beings, but all other creatures. Shiva-consciousness is all-pervading. "With hands, feet, eyes, head, mouth and ears pervading everything, He permeates the entire Universe."

All that we witness is Shiva Consciousness; nothing else. Shiva does not mean a particular form with matted hair and tiger skin. Wherever we look and whichever form we come across – whether a child or an elderly person, whether a woman or a man, in every form Shiva Consciousness is resplendent.

How can you describe the all-pervading Shiva-consciousness or limit it to a particular time and place? God is described by different people in diverse ways depending on their imagination and understanding. But the nameless, formless God is omnipresent and all-pervading.

Who can describe such Divinity? There is only one sign for Divinity, that is, Consciousness. In whichever form this Divine Consciousness permeates, it will assume that form – it may be the form of a dog, a crow, a crane or a human being.

All that you witness in this objective world is a manifestation of Shiva. It pervades the three worlds; earth, space and nether world and exists in the three periods of time; past, present and future. It is indescribable.

Just like Ramana Maharshi, who worshiped Shiva's mountain, Sathya Sai Baba also recognized the importance of Mount Arunachala when, as a young boy of 14, he sat on a boulder and chanted: "Om Namah Shivaya, Shivaya Namah Om, Arunachala Shiva, Arunachala Shiva, Arunachala Shiva Aruna Shiv Om". Sri Sathya Sai Baba often told devotees to go to Arunachala and, just like Ramana Maharshi, would encourage them to follow the method of Self Enquiry: "All agitation will cease the moment one enters on the enquiry. 'Who am I?' This was the sadhana that Ramana Maharshi achieved and taught to his disciples. This is also the easiest of all disciplines."

Sai Baba also taught that the 'I' is an illusion like the water of a river that is caught between its banks but has forgotten the vastness of the ocean of divinity. If we can free ourselves from the limited thought of 'I' we can realize this divinity and know for certain that we are not the impermanent body but, in reality, are the eternal Atma.

In an interview with forty Western devotees on April 1st, 1985, he was asked how we could reach this state: "Through love, only through love. Love is everything. Love is God. Live in love. Start the day with love, spend the day with love, fill the day with love and end the day with love. That is the way to God."

Glimpses of Arunachala

We arrived eventually at Thiruvannamalai and could see the sacred mountain, Arunachala, reaching above the town. The town's name, Thiruvannamalai, means in Tamil "Reverend Inaccessible Mountain" but Arunachala itself, in reality, is a high hillock but considered by everyone to be a mountain of spirituality. The name Arunachala comes from the Sanskrit and literally means 'Unmoving Morning Star' and sometimes is called the 'red mountain' due to its reddish hue. In legend Aruna, the morning star, is the charioteer of the Sun god, Surya, who rides across the sky in a chariot yoked to seven magnificent white horses. I could tell, even from my first glimpse of the mountain as my heart unexpectedly welled into my mouth, that this was no ordinary place. I could already feel the timeless majesty of its spirit beckoning me to the summit.

When we got to our hotel we met in my room, with its incredible view of Arunachala against a cobalt blue sky, and Mr. Prakash described the itinerary of events that he had planned. This was another of those occasions where Simon and I were so desperately tired that we were speaking gibberish ourselves and it was even harder to understand exactly what was being said in these heavy Indian dialects.

"So are we walking up the mountain or around the mountain tomorrow or are we visiting the Ramana ashram?" I ask.

"Whoever you want. This hotel is better but all at once would be too much," comes the perplexing reply. After a few more surreal instructions our best guess was that we were to be up early in the morning and then climb the mountain and then, the day after, that we would again rise early to walk around the mountain.

"Did you get all that Simon?" I say after the charming two men leave the room. "You were nodding and I assume you understood."

"Not a word of it," smirks Simon. "I'm not sure if we need sandals or climbing gear but I guess we'll find out soon enough."

"What was all that business about borrowing lawnmowers from a man in Nairobi?"

"Your guess is as good as mine," he replies. "I heard something different but it was just as weird."

Walking up the Arunachala and around it were part of the process of building our spiritual energy before we start the remedies, some of which would be done at the huge Annamalaiyar Temple located at the base of the mountain. Clearly there would be some interesting scenery to view so we agreed that Simon would take the heavy camera – the Red.

The entrance to the path to the top of Arunachala is through the back of the Ramana Maharishi ashram but we had been told, at the hotel and from other sources, that we would not be able to get access as the route had been closed for some months while tree plantings were being done as part of the Arunachala reforestation project. Remarkably, as we entered the ashram, a decision had been made that day to open the path and Mr. Prakash was excited and amazed that we had arrived at exactly the right time as the door was opened for the first time in months. He took this as an extremely fortuitous omen.

It did all feel that we were somehow moving in perfect synchronization with the cosmic tide. Tuning into history at Mahabalipuram had already tuned me in to the vibrations of India. Anyone who has worked as a psychic or even sat in a development circle will know how, when a person becomes psychically open, they become like a sponge that absorbs both the good and bad energy emitted from spirits, auras, people, objects and places. Here I became immediately aware of being soaked in spiritual energy. It is hard to describe to anyone who is not already sensitive to these things but I had an elated feeling of being lifted by the energy of the place – and we had not even taken our first steps onto the mountain itself. This is not fantasy or wishful fancy but places like Arunachala really can pick up a spiritually sensitive person and do something to their soul. It is not just psychics and mediums who feel these things – it is something that anyone who is open and receptive can experience. It is said that Shiva concealed His resplendent luminous form by manifesting Himself into the Arunachala. He said: "As the moon derives its light from the sun, so other holy places shall derive their sanctity from Arunachala. This is the only place where I have taken this form for the benefit of those who wish to worship me and obtain illumination. Arunachala is OM itself. I will appear on the summit of this hill every year at Kartigai in the form of a peace-giving beacon."

We walked most of the path to the top in silence and took in the energy of the place. I felt a little sorry for Simon who was lugging a heavy camera and rushing ahead to take shots of our ascent. Everything that was happening was beyond the reach of the camera for this was an inner transformation. Our narrative was within and with God. My thoughts turned to my life story and my life's purpose and I enjoyed the flow of ideas and feelings that were spontaneously emerging from my unconscious as we took the gentle walk to the summit. During the three hours it takes to get to the top I had a strong feeling that the spirit world was close to me. In particular my thoughts were with the spirit of my grandfather who, as a young man of 15 at the time of the First World War, had been posted to Nigeria to map its unexplored areas. (He'd lied about his age when he joined the army.) He would have loved all this. I remembered his stories about mapping sacred hills in Africa that were considered taboo and haunted by the natives. He would take his life in his hands by daring to step on those sacred Voodoo hills. I felt his spirit close to me and urging me on to complete my spiritual journey. With every step Arunachala seemed to be opening me to spiritual things.

At the top is a small building – more of a hut really – where people can sit inside, meditate and allow the mountain to work its magic. I stepped inside from the bright light of the hillside and fumbled around to find a place on the concrete floor where I could sit and meditate. By now I was what we psychics call 'open' with my aura, chakras and spirit, in a state of complete receptivity. Here the miraculous energy of the mountain could percolate as I dived deep into meditation.

The meditation room at the top is called Skandashram and is close to the cave, where Bhagwan Ramana Maharshi lived from 1916 to 1922. Skanda means 'spurting or spilling' in Sanskrit and is also the name of the god of war, also known as Murugan. As I sat, the thought came to me that Sharavana Baba – whom I wrote about in *Messages from the Universe* – had told me that I would visit this ashram. It seemed as if everything was unfolding exactly as it should. This is a strange and hard to describe feeling but, once you start doing the remedies in the Naadi, all sorts of strange feelings and coincidences start to happen. This has been my experience and was also reported by others who have consulted the Naadi and set about changing their destiny.

I had immersed myself so deeply in my mediation that, by the time I emerged, I was feeling drunk with the divine energy. When Simon pointed the camera at me and asked me to describe how I was feeling I discovered that it was near impossible to talk. Fortunately he understood exactly how I was feeling as we were all being swept away with the power of the place. I spluttered out a few words to camera and we began our descent.

This feeling of being upheld by a hidden energy remained throughout the day and reverberated throughout my stay in India. At times, now, when I sit to meditate at home, I sometimes feel the same energy there in the background of my awareness, reinforcing my spirit and aiding me on my journey through life.

A little way down from the summit there is an outcrop of rocks where we could sit and integrate the experience. From here we could see India stretching far into the pastel horizon and hear the occasional screech of a bird and the faint clatter of sound rising from the town below. Sitting majestically facing East in the midst of it all was the 11 stories high towers and courtyards of the gigantic Shiva Temple of Annamalaiyar. Conscious of the energy of everything, I felt that it had been strategically placed to maximize the flow of power emerging from the hill. It struck me that these ancient builders knew so much more than we have ever dreamed about the true nature of the world and the flow of the life force through it.

Mr. Prakash advised me that, once we had descended the hill, we needed to go to the temple where I was to have performed some of the remedies. I had noticed that, throughout this journey, he had occasionally been looking at his watch and opening his astrological almanac. Part way down Mr. Prakash said, "Stop here. Now I must give you a stone." We moved to a spot under the rustling trees where Mr. Prakash made a few chants and prayers.

"Wait, wait, wait," said Mr. Prakash as he looked at his watch and held my wrist. "Wait, wait waaaaiiiiit. Okay now is okay sir. Open your palm sir and take the stone!" He placed a stone in my hand and closed my palm. After some more chanting he explained that I had to receive the stone from the mountain when the planets – and particularly Mercury – were in the most perfect alignment on that day.

Annamalaiyar Temple

With the sun beginning to set and flushing the sky pink against the emerald leaves of the mountain trees we made the final descent and took the car to the Annamalaiyar Temple where the first remedies were to be performed. It was dark by the time we arrived at the temple. We took off our shoes and walked barefoot towards the high black towers of the temple that loomed into the rolling moonlit sky, like a rocky surrealist landscape painted by Max Ernst. Walking barefoot on the filthy Indian streets, my virgin pink toes negotiated their way over bits of broken glass, excrement and worse.

"I hope you've had a Hepatitis shot." I quipped to Simon who, I could see, was also tiptoeing along the road and balancing his camera on his shoulder.

Could I welcome everything into my heart including, perhaps, illness? But also mixed with these 'monkey mind' thoughts I could feel something deep within me opening up. The power of Arunachala had sent me into a spiritual spin that just wouldn't leave. One moment I'd be exchanging banter with Simon and the next I was lost in sudden and deep spiritual revelry.

Although I knew nothing about the temple at that time, it was apparent to me that its builders knew something about the energy of the mountain and that placing it on this exact spot was no arbitrary decision. Earlier, when we'd stood atop Arunachala, Mr. Prakash had raised his arm and pointed towards this place, saying something about straight lines. What he said made no sense to me at the time but, researching later, I discover that the Annamalaiyar Temple has been built as part of a series of five Shiva temples, known as the Pancha Bhoota Stalam, which were constructed according to Vedic sciences and sacred geometry and in a perfect, straight line.

The Annamalaiyar Temple is connected to the element of fire and aligns straight in line with Ekambareswarar Temple (Earth) at Kanchipuram, the Jambukeswara Temple (water) at Thiruvanaikaval, the Sri Kalahastheeswara Temple at Kalahasthi and the Thillai Natarajar Temple at Chidambaram. Each colossal temple connects with one of the five primary elements and they are like power centres, creating vortices of spiritual energy that envelops this sacred landscape to bring about inner transformation in those that are open to its influences. Chidambaram Natrajana Temple, Kanchipuram

Ekambareswarar Temple, Srikalahasti Temples are aligned exactly in a straight line at 79 degree 41 minutes East longitude.

All of the above and the mystical power of Arunachala open us to the possibility that the ancients were aware of an invisible energy grid that stretched across the whole planet. It is claimed by some that they understood the earth in terms of energy, frequency and vibration and could sense this in the landscape. In China, practitioners of Fung Shui Geomancy called these earth energy lines *Lung mei* which means 'dragon paths'. In the west we call them Ley Lines – a phrase that was coined in 1921 by the archaeologist Alfred Watkins and referring to alignments of mystical places of geographical and historical interest, such as ancient monuments and megaliths, natural ridge-tops and water-fords. Perhaps these ideas originated in India and were part of the knowledge passed to mankind from the sunken continent of Kumari Kandam, the mythical lost continent located south of present-day India and which I will be explaining in detail later.

Many of the world's most sacred sites sit at the meeting points of ley lines including the Pyramids of Giza, Machu Picchu, Easter Island, Lhasa Tibet, Puma Punku, Mohenjo Daro, Angkor Wat, the Nazca Lines and structures all over the world. Could it be that on mount Arunachala, and now here at the Annamalaiyar Temple, I was tuning in to something beyond the visible world that was once known to our archaic ancestors but is today quickly dismissed as pseudoscience?

With our bare feet now smarting with the grit and dust of the Thiruvannamalai streets we reached the entrance of the temple. The temple guards approached us.

"No filming here." Mr. Prakash tried his best to get us permission but, after a long conversation in Tamil, we were still not granted permission. Simon lumbered back to the car with the heavy camera and, on his return, we stepped into the temple.

Mr. Prakash tapped my knee. "Always enter the temples leading with your right foot," he explained. "This is good." The right side of the body is the 'Purusha Side' which means it is stable and spiritual. Purusha is the cosmic man or Self, Consciousness, and Universal principle and is the energy we want to use as we leave our daily life behind us.

As we stepped into the central courtyard of the temple, the scale of it became apparent. The temple complex covers 10 hectares, and is one of the largest in India. At night it looks mysterious to see its four eerie gateway towers – known as gopurams – shadowing the sky. Wherever you look there are strange carvings of gods in the walls and stone figures casting black shadows in the moonlight. As we moved deeper into the temple we heard the clatter of ceremonies, saw the flickering light of fires and could smell the scent of sandalwood incense. We moved into a dark temple area and mixed with the people whose faces were harsh shadowed in the chiaroscuro light cast by the floodlights seeping in from outside. Here Mr. Prakash arranged for a priest to perform, for a small fee, a personal Puja Archana at the shrines. This would be the first of many that I would be doing in temples across Southern India. I had done this before in Indian Temples in London when I sought the remedies for my first Naadi readings but here, enveloped by this incredible atmosphere and with the residual energy of the mountain still with me, it all felt tremendously powerful. My aura was completely open as the priest began Puja to the gods, specifically consummated for me and my family's future health and well-being.

When it was finished and we went to walk away, the priest stopped us, looked hard into my eyes and drew us back while saying something in Tamil to Mr. Prakash. Mr. Prakash spoke into my ear above the noise of the temple clatter and said "The priest says that the light of God is in your eyes and he wants to do another Puja for you. A special one so that you have a very long life and can do all of your spiritual work,"

It seemed that the priest had recognized how moved, open and vitalized I was by the whole experience and could perhaps see in me the resonating power of Mount Arunachala.

Next day we were up before dawn. It had been a hard day, climbing the mountain, and a late night at the temple, but we are to walk around the holy mountain and I'm shattered before I start. The act of walking around it is called Giri Pradakshina – 'Giri' means hill and Pradakshina refers to the act of walking around any holy place in a clockwise direction, with one's right side facing the object of worship. Doing this is said to remove sins and desires and brings freedom from rebirth. One step, they say, brings happiness in this world, a second, happiness in heaven, and a third gives the bliss of Satyaloka, the ultimate heavenly plane. It is best to walk around slowly in silent meditation or chanting a japa mantra – this is usually the recital of a divine name such as 'Om namah Shivaya'.

We start when it's dark and initially walk along the streets of Thiruvannamalai dodging the traffic in places where there's no pavement. Even though at this stage it's mainly streets and small shops there's nonetheless a feeling of the energetic presence of the mountain with every step I take. I think about the legend that says that Mount Arunachala is the place where Lord Shiva manifested as a column of light to settle the argument between the god Brahma and Vishnu. This is one of the holiest places in India where so many great saints and sages once lived in the mount's caves and in whose footsteps I am now following. I am reminded of the fact that, no matter the direction we take, walking with God will always bring us to our destination.

Most of the route is overwhelmed by noisy traffic but there are places where the path is clear and tranquil. Here it is maintained by an ashram that keeps it spotlessly clean as an act of spiritual service to the community. It's a fascinating walk but the tiredness of the past days is beginning to overtake me and, despite my best efforts, all I'm thinking about is where and when can I get a nice cup of tea?

We stop at a dhabas, or roadside tea stall, and enjoy a chai with crushed ginger or cardamom and all the troubles of the world dissolve with this, the greatest of India's legacies. Before our journey concludes, Mr. Prakash explains how we will soon be visiting the Ramana Maharshi ashram to gather enough spiritual energy in readiness for the hardest part of our remedial quest, which is to get the blessing of a Siddha yogi. For this we would have to travel into a remote place in the mountains and hope that our paths will cross. Mr. Prakash has checked his almanac and the planets will soon be in just the right alignment for us to accomplish this. The stars have given him a direction and soon we will be off to the middle of nowhere in search of the holy man.

CHAPTER 8

ॐ

Ramana Maharshi

There is what I consider to be a beautiful line in my Naadi Reading which says to listen to: "he who speaks the language of silence, him you should cherish as your own true and most happy self, for he is no other than your true liberated self." In some ways this also summarizes the teachings of Ramana Maharshi[1] who lived on Mount Arunachala and whose ashram I was to now to visit. We had briefly walked through the ashram in order to get to the entrance to the path up Mount Arunachala but now I could spend some time in the ashram itself and also learn more about Ramana Maharshi and later interview one of his most famous devotees.

The ashram is built in Tiruvannamalai at the foot of the mountain and on a busy through road. We enjoyed coffee in a shop opposite. The ashram is easily assessable and also attracts many westerners who have been inspired by the teachings of Ramana Maharshi who died on April 14, 1950. And where there are westerners you'll also find beggars. Instinctively I gave some money to an old woman who pestered me for some cash but was gently reprimanded by Mr Prakash. Although I was to do a lot of charitable work in the days ahead, giving to beggars was not recommended. Apart from the fact that we could be mobbed, it is illegal in some areas to give to street beggars because begging has grown into a gangland business. For the privilege of begging outside the ashram, each beggar must hand over their takings to the gang's leader, who takes a large cut from the pot. Beggars have also been known to maim and disfigure themselves <u>deliberately to get more money</u> and there are many scams afoot to

---

[1] Note Ramana Maharshi's name is usually spelt without the extra 'i' as in the traditional spelling of 'maharishi'.

fleece gullible westerners. The biggest problem is that begging can become more profitable than working: it disempowers people from taking up the jobs offered them by the government; they don't want to work and the problem grows.

We take our lives in our hands, cross the busy Chengam Road, step through the arched entrance and enter the ashram grounds. Immediately there is a sense of serenity and peace and an unhurried atmosphere that contrasts starkly to the bustle of the moment before. Sri Ramana Ashram, is also known as Sri Ramanasramam, and the place which was home to Ramana Maharshi from 1922. We cross a large open courtyard flanked by shady trees, one of which is a 400 year old Iluppai tree. To our left are two towers built in the traditional Dravidian style of temple architecture. One surmounts the Matrubhuteswara Shrine, erected over the tomb of Sri Maharshi's mother, and the other is over the New Hall.

Simon sets off to get some footage of the ashram while I am beckoned to the New Hall where I can sit and listen to the chanting and walk around the life-sized statue of Sri Maharshi and a large yogasana, or couch, beautifully carved from a single stone and polished to look like black marble. Before the temple ceremonies start I am able to sit for about an hour in meditation, contemplate the vibrations of the place and think about the life and teachings of Ramana Maharshi. Some of the westerners here strike me as spiritual tourists but it is important for me to connect as deeply as I can with the spirit of the place and to the message of the master who once lived here. This is part of the process needed before starting the actual remedies: to build and build the spiritual energies in my aura till my karma is ready to burst!

Where I sit I can see pictures of Ramana on the wall and a golden statue of him in the altar area. At the age of 16 Ramana had something like a 'near death experience' in which he entered into a state of divine consciousness and realized the true nature of the Self. He became aware of a divine current within him that could never die. Soon afterwards he came to this spot at the base of the holy mountain and decided to remain here for the rest of his life. For long periods of time his mind was in such a state of transcendence that he completely neglected his body and he was incessantly bitten by ants. Some people found him and realized that this was a holy man who was to become one of India's greatest spiritual teachers.

Meanwhile, as I sat in meditation, Simon had lots of time to film the setting and somehow capture its graceful ambience and peace. He gets footage of the dancing light through the ashram trees, the interesting buildings and shrines and the birds and animals that pepper the grounds. There are monkeys, white peacocks and bright coloured birds; its animal residents seem to be attracted by the peace that surrounds the ashram's buildings and grounds while we human visitors can contemplate the nature of our existence and, like Ramana, enquire who is the 'I' that is having the human experience.

Ramana Maharshi (1879 – 1950) was a Vedanta philosopher who encouraged his followers to seek the source of our experience by constantly asking ourselves the question 'Who am I?' This is a method which ultimately takes us to the infinite silence, peace and bliss that lies at the heart of our being and to our central Self that preempts thoughts, feelings and our sense separateness and personal identity. We are at heart formless, immanent-consciousness. His teaching is very simple yet incredibly profound. We are charged simply to 'be as you are.'

Ramana Maharshi expresses this idea thus: "Every living being longs to be happy; untainted by sorrow; and everyone has the greatest of love for himself; which is solely due to the fact that happiness is his real nature. Hence in order to realize that inherent and untainted happiness, which indeed he daily experiences when the mind is subdued in deep sleep, it is essential that he should know himself. For obtaining such knowledge the enquiry, "Who am I?" in the quest for the Self is the best means." Most of his teachings were given in silence and his way of helping others was through a silent outpouring of spiritual vibrations into troubled souls that many experienced as a form of direct telepathic teaching.

He was born on 30 December 1879 in Tiruchuli, Tamil Nadu, South India, with the birth name of Venkataraman Iyer, but is known to the world by his spiritual/yogic name Bhagavan Sri Ramana Maharshi. At the age of 16 he was suddenly overwhelmed with a fear of death. He was gripped by what has been described as "a flash of excitement" or "heat," like some avesam – a "current" or "force" that seemed to possess him. This epiphany moment was the catalyst for an all-enveloping line of self-enquiry in which he wrestled with the question "What is it that dies?"

In the moments that followed he realized that his true nature was imperishable and lay beyond the body, mind or personality. Bhagavan Sri Ramana Maharshi described the experience: 'When I lay down with limbs outstretched and mentally enacted the death scene and realized that the body would be taken and cremated and yet I would live, some force, call it atmic power or anything else, rose within me and took possession of me. With that, I was reborn and I became a new man. I became indifferent to everything afterwards, having neither likes nor dislikes.'

Bhagavan, I believe, had realized something far past the Spiritualist knowledge that life goes on after death; his consciousness had penetrated beyond the corporal, beyond the spirit, beyond the personality and individual soul to the vastness of infinity that is the bedrock of all our natures. By knowing what he was not, he understood directly who he really was. And this was a complete and total immersion. Unlike many of us who may get a glimpse of, or enter for a short while into, the divine state of endless being, for Bhagavan Sri Ramana Maharshi it was a permanently maintained state. Nobody came back.

After his enlightenment the young boy told no one about his experience and, for the next six weeks, endeavored to play the role of being an ordinary schoolboy. He appeared to be withdrawn and indifferent to his studies and soon was to throw away his books and expressed to his elder brother his desire to take up a life of meditation as a sadhu. He left his family and headed for the sacred mountain of Arunachala. As I have explained already, this mountain at Thiruvannamalai is considered by Hindus to be extremely sacred and legends say that it appeared when Lord Shiva manifested as a column to settle a dispute between Brahma the creator god, and Vishnu the preserver god. Many holy people had spent their lives meditating in its caves and, from that point on, Ramana Maharshi refused ever to travel more than two miles from its base. Initially at the nearby temples, and then for 17 years secluded in a cave, Ramana Maharshi spent the rest of his life immersed in the vibrations of this sacred mountain – the vibrations of which, he believed, triggered and sustained his spiritual state. His birth name Venkataraman Iyer was dropped and his growing circle of followers now proclaimed him to be Bhagavan Sri Ramana Maharshi.

The death of his mother in 1922 served as a second major catalyst in his life. As she lay dying Ramana put his right hand on her heart, on the right side of the chest, and his left hand on her head, for hours and until her death. From 1922 till his death in 1950 Ramana lived in Sri Ramanasramam, the ashram that developed around his mother's tomb.

Like many westerners I first read about Ramana Maharshi in the bestselling book published in 1934 *Search in Secret India* by Paul Brunton (real name Raphael Hurst) who left a journalistic career to live among yogis, mystics, and holy men, and studied Eastern and Western esoteric teachings. Brunton describes his encounter at the ashram in 1931: "I fold a thin cotton blanket upon the floor and sit down, gazing expectantly at the silent figure in such a rigid attitude upon the couch... If he is aware of my presence, he betrays no hint, gives no sign. His body is supernaturally quiet, as steady as a statue. Not once does he catch my gaze, for his eyes continue to look into remote space, and infinitely remote it seems."

Brunton expected something to happen but the yogi simply remained in a blissful meditation that had the power to draw everyone present into its power. Eventually Ramana gazed at Paul Brunton who said of the encounter: "His eyes shine with astonishing brilliance. Strange sensations begin to arise in me. Those lustrous orbs seem to be peering into the inmost recesses of my soul... I become aware that he is definitely linking my own mind with his, that he is provoking my heart into that state of starry calm which he seems perpetually to enjoy."

Through Paul Brunton's book, Ramana Maharshi became one of the first Indian gurus to become widely known to a western readership and excerpts are still published and distributed by Ramana's ashram. Some years after its publication Brunton fell out with the ashram administrators, saying that there were threats of violence against him, and he was eventually forced to leave the ashram. There had been disagreements between Brunton and Ramana's brother concerning a newspaper article that Brunton had written but, above all, Brunton felt that the administrators of the ashram had become arrogant and had a "holier than thou attitude" and Ramana Maharshi, he said, was not exercising any proper control over the organization.

From a spiritual perspective Brunton did not like the fact that the teachings discouraged engagement with life. He believed that it was not sufficient for a realized person just to meditate but that they should engage with the outside world. At the time, World War II was imminent and Ramana Maharshi took absolutely no interest in world events or the reported atrocities. Brunton also criticizes Ramana Maharshi's teaching that 'even God is an illusion' and, having hailed from a Theosophist/Spiritualist background, did not like the way Ramana Maharshi dismissed siddhis. (Psychic phenomena.)

For many of us Westerners some of the ideas from the East are hard to understand. What is real and what is illusion and whether all things – including the sense of 'I' – have inherent existence or not are difficult ideas to take onboard. Phenomena are real and have existence but perhaps not quite in the way we think they do.

Most westerners think we are the product of our thoughts, feelings and memories but, according to Ramana Maharshi, as all these things can be observed then it is not our true self. And, for a spiritualist medium like me, who spends their time proving that the sense of personality survives physical death, there are many difficult questions that these non-dualist philosophies pose, which I will address later in this book.

Ramana Maharshi tells us that the 'I' is an illusion: "Is there a mind in the first place? What you call mind is an illusion. It starts from the 'I'-thought. Without the gross or subtle senses, you cannot be aware of the body or the mind. Still, it is possible for you to be without these senses. In such a state, you are either asleep or aware of the Self only. Awareness of Self is ever there. Remain what you truly are and this question will not arise." [2]

What he describes here as the 'Self' – with a capital S – is the absolute existence that is described in philosophy as 'non-duality': the idea that the universe and all its multiplicity are ultimately expressions or appearances of one essential reality. The Self is that absolute reality, that many think of as God – not as something separate but as an all-inclusive oneness where there is no difference between the relative world and "absolute" reality. This is the basis of the Advaita Vedanta school of Indian Philosophy: that the true Self, Atman, is the same as the highest Reality, Brahman. Through self-enquiry we can come to realize that even our sense of 'I' is one with the absolute and with this realization the illusion falls away and we achieve moksha – spiritual liberation. From a Spiritualist's viewpoint this means that even the soul that persists into the afterlife is seen as an illusion for it becomes known that Brahman (the Absolute) is the only reality and that this world and the next are unreal and that the individual soul (Jiva) is non-different from Brahman.

I am not this body, I am not this mind, I am not a medium, I am not Craig Hamilton-Parker: I am 'I'. I am the true limitless Self. As we all are. To get to absolute understanding of this we must engage in relentless self-enquiry. We need to watch ourselves and ask questions about the true nature of the self. In this way, the illusion of Maya will disappear when the truth flashes like lightning across the heart and mind and we know existence as it is. We wake up from the dreams and nightmares we have conjured up from our ignorance and desires. This is the path of knowledge, which is brought about when the mind and heart are purified through spiritual practices, devotion and surrender. With the end of illusion and delusion so ends pain and suffering.

---

[2] From Talks with Ramana Maharshi, recorded June 29th, 1936.

CHAPTER 9

ॐ

David Godman

I returned to the ashram later as Kim Paisol had arranged for me to interview David Godman, one of the world's top authorities on Ramana Maharshi. He was educated at Oxford University and, in the last 30 years, has written or edited 16 books on topics related to Sri Ramana, his teachings and his followers. For many years he was the librarian of the ashram and, although Ramana had died three years before he was born, David Godman was able to get to know many of Ramana's direct disciples. One of his best-known books is his edited anthology of Ramana Maharshi's teachings, *Be As You Are*, that was published by Penguin in 1985 and which, coincidentally, I had just finished reading a few days before setting off to India.

David agreed to an interview and had no problem with my including it in this book but he did not want to be filmed for the TV program. Although this was disappointing, it was perhaps for the best as, even with a documentary format, TV demands a fast pace and his carefully considered and intelligent replies to my questions would probably not fit the bill. We could enjoy the discussion and take our time as others gathered around us to listen to us.

Craig: There are a few things I would like to ask, also on a somewhat personal level about Ramana and some of the things I understand and also maybe don't understand. First of all his concept of the 'I'. As I understand it he is explaining it a little like the Buddha did in that the 'I' is empty of inherent existence: basically that there is no self. So my question is: 'Is there such a thing as an individual self?'

David: From the absolute standpoint not at all but what he says is that there is something that identifies with the body, that pretends it occupies the body, that projects an exterior world outside of itself and that it sees that world and sustains its belief in its reality by continuous association with external objects.

Craig: So what is it that's pretending?

David: If I give you the underlying structure we can discuss and go on from that. He says that the idea that you are an individual person is created and sustained by association; that this thing called 'I', that you imagine yourself to be, will only exist if you register a sense impression or have a thought so there then becomes a subject-I, which perceives or thinks about an object, which is separate from itself.

Craig: So is that dependent upon the body?

David: It's dependent upon having an idea that you are a person. We can backtrack to that later. So he said that this sense of being a person is entirely contingent on this thought that you have about yourself being 'I' connecting to a thought of something that is separate from the 'I'. So if you see, perceive or think something then there is an internally created 'I' which has that thought which perceives that perception. So what he is saying is that the reality of this 'I' can be challenged by disassociating it from all the things that it automatically jumps out to and connects with. So he said that if you put continuous attention on this sense of 'I', which is the centre of your thoughts, the perceiver of your perceptions, and stop it connecting with all the exterior phenomena that you want to experience and enjoy, then that individuality can no longer exist; it has to withdraw and disappear and then you can realize its inherent unreality and it goes.

Craig: My spiritual work is as a Spiritualist and I work as a medium, giving proof of life after death, and my objective in life has always been to prove the continuation of the personality after death in order to give comfort to people who are bereaved; so how does the sense of 'I' continue after death and has Bhagavan spoken about this?

David: He says that the mechanism and the fuel that drives the whole process, what you call vasanas – You understand vasanas?

Craig: Yes, latent tendencies.

David: Vasanas are the inherent tendencies and desires that cause your mind to extrovert and enjoy something. They are the desires that you feel an impulsion to fulfil. So he said that, at the end of the physical existence of the body, all of these vasanas are not extinguished; the body ceases but the vasanas withdraw into the heart, into the self, where they remain latent for a while and, because there's an energy in them, which demands expression and enjoyment, at some later point they create a new body and a new world in which they can continue to enjoy desire and experience through a new form. So what continues is not something called an 'I', it's all the unfulfilled desires that you had when you died last time and that they create a new world, a new body, a new environment and into which they can be expressed and enjoyed again.

Craig: So to summarize, the 'I' is the persistence of the vasanas?

David: The 'I' is something, all of these things come up, it's created a body; you see a world and then you say 'I am this person in this world'. But, if you go a level back, it's the vasanas which have brought the body into existence. To a certain extent they have created the world you see outside of you and, simultaneously with that, you say 'I see this world; I live in this world'. So the 'I' is created as a kind of adjunct to this process of creation whereby the vasanas take form and manifest again so that you can experience and fulfil the desires you haven't got rid of.

Craig: One other question on a slightly different angle that I'd like to ask about is that I've also been a follower of Sathya Sai Baba, and some of his devotees have claimed that Sathya Sai Baba came to see Ramana when he was a young man. Is there any evidence of that?

David: There is no evidence at this end but he told this story that he came here when he was a thirteen year old boy – I think that would be 1939 – and apparently this is entirely his recollections, so it's not supported by any accounts here. Apparently bhagavan patted him on the head and said 'you're a good boy', or something like, this after which he composed his first bhajan (song), which contained Arunachala Shiva as the refrain. So that's the story from his end but there's no evidence of this at this end that he came – though I'm not disputing it – I'm just saying that's his story but there is no record of his visit here.

Craig: Also while I've been here I've consulted the Naadi leaves. I believe Bhagavan Ramana's leaves were found in the past but he rejected the idea of his leaves being read?

David: Somebody found the collection that pertained to him. They've been published and you can go to the library here and ask them and they will show them to you. They seem quite reliable up to the moment when the person said 'these are your leaves' and then after that they tend to stray further and further from what happened later in his life so I find that a bit suspect.

We chatted for a while after the recorded interview but a few other interesting ideas emerged as we talked. David asked me about my travels in India and was pleased to hear that I had walked around Mount Arunachala. "Bhagavan was very non-prescriptive. He would never tell anyone to do anything, with one exception: he said walk around the hill. He'd never tell you 'do this practice' or 'stop doing that practice' unless you specifically pushed him for a decision but the one thing he would often say, unasked, is walk around the hill. People would say 'this is irrational, why what's the point?' and he said 'I know it's irrational; just do it and see and when you get back you'll want to do it again.'

Craig: It is such an energetic place. I read somewhere that some say it was once a volcano? Is that a fallacy?

David: It's igneous rock buried a long way under the ground so, if you want an analogy: if you have a liquid magma, if it cools very quickly you have very tiny crystals that you can't see. For example obsidian is just stuff that comes out of a volcano, cools in the air and drops as glass so there's no crystals. Then, if it's like basalt on the flow, you get a magnifying glass out and you can see tiny little crystals: that's the lava stuff but it's stuff that comes up from the centre of the earth and it takes hundreds of millions of years to crystalize. Then you get the visible crystals and that's your granite. So they form a long way under the crust and then, by uplift and erosion, slowly they come to the surface.

Craig: In my heart, and there's no proof, but I felt the whole place was like a giant subterranean Shiva Lingam.

David: Well that's like the mythology of this place. Shiva appeared as a giant column of light to settle a dispute between Brahma and Vishnu and, at the end, he was requested to condense himself into a physical form because the light was too dazzling to see. So he agreed and just reformed himself into this particular mountain. So it's not a place where he lives, or some story in his life, but the tradition is that this place is Shiva himself in the form of a rock.

Craig: So I guess my intuitive feeling is right. It has a transformative power, almost like a spiritual alchemy happens from that energy. Did Ramana ever speak of his past life?

David: Very limited hints but he made a point of not giving out information like that. He did say once, he gave a long philosophical explanation, of some topic that someone had asked a question on, and then he sighed and said 'thank God my poor samskaras – past life tendencies – took me straight to enquiry otherwise I would have got lost in all this philosophy. The implication to me is that he was someone doing self-enquiry in his past life and that it was unfinished business and that, this time around, he asked the questions once and got the answer. So when he said 'my previous samskaras took me straight to enquiry' I think that he was saying that this was my unfinished practice from a past life and this time I only asked it once and got the right answer straight away.

Craig: So he'd been enquiring before unless his last remaining samskara was the tendency to self-enquiry.

David: He said he had a very strong tendency to enquiry, which manifested on the day of his liberation. He asked himself once and he got the right answer. That was his whole business in this life.

Craig: So he wasn't an avatar in that respect?

David: People said he was the avatar of Subrahmanya, which he never accepted, but, interestingly, he didn't mind what you thought of him but he would never confirm or deny it. So, had he said 'no it's nonsense it's not true', then people wouldn't have persisted with this idea. But it was a very common idea, particularly the first two decades of the last century, and it gained expression in a text called Ramana Gita, which was written by Ganapati Muni, and he had him down as having three previous lifetimes: one was as the avatar of Subrahmanya, then as a philosopher called Kumarila Bhatta, a contemporary of Adi-Sankaracharya, and then as Nyanda Sambanda, a Tamil saint. So this was Ganapati's idea but Bhagavan laughed at that and said that it is simply not possible because the chronology was wrong. But the idea that he was Subrahmanya is a persistent one. He didn't mind if people treated him or assumed him to be that because he thought it was good for their devotion.

End of Interview

It was a little disappointing that David Goodman had preferred not to be filmed as he is a very interesting man and someone who can very clearly explain the teachings of Ramana that many westerners would find very hard to understand. David is a person of great intellect who speaks from the heart with great clarity and compassion.

One of the simplest lessons I have learnt from Ramana is that intellectual gymnastics will get you nowhere. Kim summarized it when he sent me my Naadi reading saying: 'If you can learn to remain within in peace and happiness, then all else will manifest by itself in accordance with karma and without a worry. The main thing is to seek within, the world will take care of itself, even though many people of the west find that very hard to understand.'

Ramana Maharshi's teaching is not new; it comes from the traditions of the Vedas where we are told that the only question that matters is "Koham?" Koh in Sanskrit means 'who' and Aham means 'I' (who am I?). If we ask ourselves this question the layers of illusion will gradually fall away.

We may engage in all sorts of intellectual gymnastics but the Vedas also offers us a simple answer which is hidden so close that we cannot see it. Koham may be on our lips but the answer to the question is on our breath. In traditional meditation we are told to watch the breath and we will sense the mantra 'SoHam'. With the inhale we hear 'so' and the exhale 'ham'. SoHam means "I am He". So, in other words, the answer to the question Koham? is SoHam! Who am I? Answer: I am He – the infinite bliss of God. So now we have the answer. But can we *realize* the answer?

CHAPTER 10

ॐ

The Siddha Yogis

The writers of the Naadi are sometimes described as Siddhas. This Sanskrit word means 'one who is accomplished' and is given to the most advanced yogis who have achieved the highest physical goals of yoga and found enlightenment. Siddha yogis usually also display extraordinary paranormal powers and have powerful psychic abilities called siddhis. When Mr. Prakash looked into my Naadi remedies we were told that we next needed to seek out a living Siddha yogi and obtain his blessing. The oracle gave him some clues as to where to go to find a Siddha yogi but it was a remote mountain location and the yogi whom Mr. Prakash had in mind had not been seen for over a year.

The eighteen enlightened Siddhas, who had written the Naadi leaves under the guidance of Lord Shiva, foresaw that humankind would fall into ignorance as the Age of Kali Yuga cast its shadow over the Earth. They saw that, in our modern times, man would become so deluded by the things of this world that he would forget his spiritual nature and so they devised the Naadi astrological system as a way to bring people back to the knowledge of their true, divine nature.

They knew, also, that from the chaos and materialism of the modern era, people's hearts would begin to yearn for the truth and seek to know what is beyond this limited world. So they devised a personalized system so that every individual could know the history of their soul and the role that it must play in this present incarnation.

Whoever is destined to consult the Naadi oracle will find their way to it – the word Naadi in Tamil means, 'to seek' or, more literally, 'destined to come on own accord.'

The Siddhas chronicled the information in the leaves to reveal the way forward and the mistakes we have made in respect of our duties, and so learn why we are facing problems in our lives today. In the remedies we are given ways to overcome these problems. The superficial seeker consults the leaves in order to overcome a problem in their life but the wise seeker will understand that the leaves also offer us a way to liberation from suffering through the direct knowledge of God. The Siddhas could see the cosmic plan and, through the leaves, prescribed remedies of Karma and devotion so that all beings could find enlightenment.

The Siddhas acquired eight main paranormal powers called the Ashta Maha Siddhis. These eight paranormal powers are as follows:

- Anima: reducing one's body even to the size of an atom
- Mahima: expanding one's body to an infinitely large size
- Garima: becoming infinitely heavy
- Laghima: becoming almost weightless
- Prapti: having unrestricted access to all places
- Prakamya: realizing whatever one desires
- Istva: possessing absolute lordship
- Vastva: the power to subjugate all

These Siddha yogis are also known as the Maharishis. This is an anglicized spelling of the Sanskrit word Maharsi (formed from the prefix maha- meaning 'great' and rsi meaning 'seer') They were known as the 'Maharshis' that is 'great seers'. With their transcendental powers they sensed and understood the microcosm and the macrocosm and could achieve miraculous insights that are beyond the grasp of normal people. They could naturally know the three dimensions of time that is past, present and future. They were also masters in Ayurvedic medicine, science, astrology and self-defense.

Many also claim that the writers of the Naadis are the Saptarishi – the seven sages/rishis who are mentioned in the Vedas and Hindu literature. They are recognized as the mind-borne sons of the creator Brahma. The 'Satapatabrahmana' gives their names as, Vashishta, Kashyapa, Viswamitra, Jamadagni, Gautama, Bharadwaja and Atri. The Vayupurana adds the eighth name of 'Bhrigu', but the congregation is still called 'Saptarishi'. (Later in this book I consult the Bhrigu Astrology Oracle which is another mind-boggling text that is similar to the Naadis.)

I consider myself supremely fortunate to have found my Naadi prediction that has my path and now revealed how I can find a living Siddha yogi to help me further. The Naadi leaves had spoken to me just like an enlightened guru who knew all the foibles, potentials and hopes of my innermost self. How lucky I have been to be shown ways to reduce the negative effects of my past karma and be forewarned of how to prevent future negative karma.

Simply to be in a position to consult the real Naadi is to have the blessings of the ancients. For reasons known only to the Siddhas, a leaf may refuse to give a reading and others never find their leaf. When I consulted the Jeeva Naadi to find a cure for a sick member of our family, the oracle knew about him and the illness but said that no remedy was available. The remedy is a form of penance, an atonement for past life sins that shows us how to escape the grip of karma. In my family member's case – a good person – he was given no magic formula and endured the horrors of a terrible debilitating illness that lasted for over a year. I was so fortunate that not only had I found my leaves and been given the remedies but now the path was leading me to seek out an enlightened Siddha who, I hoped, could perhaps clarify what was happening to me and maybe confirm my destiny.

We'd been travelling up and down India for about 10 days visiting temples and doing the prescribed rituals. We'd been getting up early and driving many miles and sometimes staying up late into the night whenever the car broke down. Perhaps one of the greatest wonders of India is the fact that we easily found a garage that was prepared to fix the car in the middle of the night. We were all getting very weary even though some of the scenery we'd been watching was awe inspiring – the sun setting over the sea, a forest fire raging over a mountain side at night, soft green paddy fields, magical temples silhouetted against amber skies… With tiredness and the call of sleep so close, it was like driving through a dream.

We stopped for chai alfresco at a filthy roadside café and Simon and I blearily took in our surroundings. The café was made out of old corrugated iron and looked like something out of the apocalyptic movie *Mad Max*. A woman was spraying what looked like petrol over the dusty ground in what appeared to us like a possible insurance job for a failing business but turned out to be simply a way of keeping the dust down. We were so tired that we were now giggling like kids at just about everything: the scabby dog sitting by the cake stand, the flies on the food, the unwashed saliva-stained glasses, the broken benches and the horrible smell of sewerage. "I wonder if they have a loyalty card?" I asked.

The next day we set off specifically to look for the Siddha yogi that Mr. Prakash believed would appear for us. The Siddha yogi he had in mind lived in a cave in the mountains near Gudiyatham. According to both the Naadi and Mr. Prakash's astrology almanac we should meet him today even though this reclusive aesthetic had not been seen by anyone for over six months. It was as if Mr. Prakash was using the Naadi and his almanac as a sort of spiritual satnav to get us to a specific but hitherto unknown destination. He was absolutely confident that we'd find him.

Now the driving was getting much more exciting as we drove along rough and dirt track roads across wild landscapes. We headed towards the Mahadevan Malai temple atop the mountains near Gudiyatham then 'Bang! Pop! Splutter…. The car came to a halt on a dirt tracked road on the hillside as steam billowed from the engine. We stepped out of the car, bare-footed and would walk the last part of the way to the temple on the scorching ground.

"Nothing to worry about," says Mr. Prakesh, "Everything will be very good, very good." No sooner had he spoken when the Siddha yogi appeared and, to our utter amazement, brushed between us. He'd come from behind us so it seemed as if he had just appeared, alone, out of the undergrowth by the side of the road. We were on the exact right spot at the place he would arrive to walk, unescorted, to the temple where, presumably, some of the closer devotees were expecting him.

This was all very auspicious and Mr. Prakash was hugely pleased that we appeared, again, to be in complete synchronization as spiritual events unfolded. We had taken a chance at seeing him and had arrived at the perfect spot for his long awaited return after nearly a year. We were the first people to get his darshan. (Glimpse of the deity.) I walked immediately just behind him as we headed silently towards the temple that was still under construction. Meanwhile, Simon grabbed the camera and ran ahead so that he could capture it all on video. For me it felt like a powerful spiritual moment and we caught it all. You could never have planned this. It just happened as it was supposed to.

Meeting Maha Ananda Siddha

This siddha yogi's name is Maha Ananda Siddha, which means 'great bliss yogi', and is indeed an extraordinary looking man. His hair is long and matted into a great mesh of tangles atop his head and he has a long straggly beard. He wears just a simple sarong around the waist and is covered from head to foot in ash. The whites of his eyes are a cadmium red and appear fierce and aflame. Having never seen pictures of this man and not knowing quite what to expect, his sudden appearance came as a shock. It was like encountering a Martian.

Of course I have since been able to learn a lot more about Maha Ananda Siddha. Just like St Francis of Assisi, who abandoned a life of luxury, so too Maha Ananda Siddha gave up his successful turmeric business to follow the spiritual path. He had already been sponsoring renovation work in many temples in Tamil Nadu and had been doing a lot of work feeding the poor until he had a life transforming encounter at midnight of December 25, 2002. In front of him stood Lord Shiva who revealed his destiny and said "You are very fortunate in this life; you are a siddha with a boon to live for a 500 years. Go to Mahadeva Mount and live in a cave there, worship Me and protect the devotees."

When he finished saying these words Shiva vanished and Maha Ananda Siddha left immediately for Mahadeva mount. Here Lord Shiva appeared again and said "You should brush your teeth and take a bath only on the first day of Chithirai. You should not seek alms from anyone. All the wealth will be heaped here. You should protect all the living creatures in this mountain from disease and suffering. From now on you should not eat food to satisfy your hunger or drink water to quench your thirst." Again Lord Shiva disappeared after giving this advice.

Maha Ananda Siddha is a comfortable build yet it is claimed that he has never eaten or drank water since this vision. Clearly, this is hard to believe yet his devotees are adamant that he has never eaten or drunk anything since 2003. One of the main parts of his mission is to help people with miracle cures brought about by the use of herbs. He is said to have cured people who had incurable diseases and can make barren women fertile by giving them Vibhuti ash. He also works closely with doctors who have a spiritual perspective and offer free medical services to the poor.

We followed Maha Ananda Siddha into the temple to a frantic commotion from the devotees at seeing their guru after such a long absence. Maha Ananda Siddha initially made a clockwise walk around the outside of the temple complex, walking into every shrine and standing there as people beat drums and chanted as loudly as they could. The place exploded in a Bedlam of chaotic clatter and noise as fires were lit, offerings made and incense burned at every shrine. At one point we all stopped and everyone smashed hundreds of coconuts onto the ground before a shrine. This is called narikel (coconut) Puja and symbolizes the sacrifice of the ego so that the sweetness may be revealed.

The spiritual mayhem lasted about an hour, concluding with an Aarati at the heart of the temple that involved masses of flaming wicks soaked in ghee as well as incense and other bowls of fire. It came to a crescendo of flames, smoke and excitement as Maha Ananda Siddha crawled through a cave-like shrine that was dramatically lit by the dancing yellow and orange lights from the fires. I've taken part in Aarati before but never on this scale and with such fervor.

Afterwards we were all given prasad (blessed food). It was a huge and tasty meal given by someone who never eats or drinks. As we walked away we looked at the fire-pit to one side of the temple. This is where Maha Ananda Siddha demonstrates his super-human powers by lying and sleeping in a roaring fire. Now this sounds crazy to most of us but the Indians telling me about all of this describe it as if it's an everyday occurrence. They let me look at the ash filled fire area where he lies down to sleep in the flames. It is a type of grate with a decorative metalwork surround made of iron tridents. This is not simple fire-walking that can be explained by modern physics that shows that the amount of time the foot is in contact with the ground is not enough to induce a burn, combined with the fact that embers are not good conductors of heat. In the case of Maha Ananda Siddha, he actually lies unmoving in a full-on roaring fire and not just in the charcoal embers. I was puzzling over all this when Mr. Prakash ran over to me and grabbed my by the arm:

"Hurry, hurry swami wants to talk to you. A few people have been called to touch his feet. Hurry or the moment will pass."

Simon frantically prepared the movie camera as we dash to a caged area of the temple where Maha Ananda Siddha stands, as a man in front of me touches his feet. "What's happening?" I whisper to Mr Prakash.

"He's telling this man in Tamil that he is a business man and that not to worry. Things will get better with his finances and also soon his daughter will be married."

Maha Ananda Siddha was standing on a slightly raised floor area and I knelt to touch his feet, hoping to get a message, but he seemed to be completely ignoring me and was shouting in Tamil at someone across the room. After a short while a devotee moved me on to allow the next person to touch the feet. As I moved away I saw Maha Ananda Siddha call Mr Prakash aside and started to talk to him at length.

"What was all that shouting about?" I asked Mr Prakash when he returned to us. He was beaming.

"Oh he was telling off a young boy across the room who was being sarcastic. He told him to go and meditate, but not at this ashram. Go somewhere far away from here. And he has a message for you that I will tell you when we get away from this noise."

Mahavatar Babaji. The drawing was ordered by Paramahamsa Yogananda, and was executed by his brother, Sananda Lal Ghosh

Mahavatar Babaji

The Siddha yogis are supreme masters of yoga, have contributed to India's knowledge of traditional medicine alchemy and chemistry, and have written many of the most important palm leaf manuscripts. They are the only people who fully understand and are able to unlock the secret meanings of many of the texts and poems of ancient India. A great deal of their knowledge relates to the doctrines that allow a person to extend their lifespan indefinitely. Some of these texts and records remain closely-guarded and secret.

Maha Ananda Siddha was born in Dharmapuri district on December 6, 1930 but claims that he will live for hundreds of years.

There are Siddha yogis who are said to have lived for many thousands of years – the most famous being the immortal yogi Babaji described in Paramahansa Yogananda's book *Autobiography of a Yogi*. Babaji, also known as Kriya Babaji Nagaraj (king of serpents) and Mahavatar Babaji, is said to be living today in the Himalayas. In his book *The Second Coming of Christ*, Yogananda states that Jesus Christ went to India and conferred with Mahavatar Babaji. This would make Babaji at least 2000 years old!

Siddha Tradition and Agastyar

Tamils claim that the Siddha tradition began millions of years ago when Lord Shiva initiated his consort Pravati Devi into a special technique for the control of breathing and the body's life force in the spinal column. This was taught in a huge cave at Amarnath in the Kashmir – the same place that a holy man had left the instructions for me to receive the Shiva Lingam that I spoke about earlier in this book. Eighteen others were later initiated on Mount Kailas in Tibet including Agastyar who is said to be the primary author of the Naadi leaves and who transcribed Shiva's prophecies. Agastyar is considered to be the first Siddha and was one of the seven sages (or Saptarishi) as mentioned in the Vedic texts. The legends say he was the son of the god Brahma of the Hindu creation story. He is said to be the father of the Tamil Language and grammar.

Agastyar was to initiate Babaji into the techniques of Kriya and medicine to enable him to attain spiritual perfection and, with this, the option of physical immortality. They entered states of consciousness and being that are beyond normal human comprehension and remain with us in physical form to assist humanity to evolve towards divine knowledge. Some of these Kriya techniques were passed down through the lineage to Paramahansa Yogananda via Lahiri Mahasaya and Swami Sri Yukteswar and are today taught by the *Self-Realization Fellowship*. I practice similar techniques given to me by another spiritual teacher and from direct inner guidance given by my spirit guides. Just as Sai Baba may come to people in dreams, so too, the Siddha yogis will make themselves known to devotees through dreams, during meditation and occasionally by materialization. No one can be enlightened by anyone else but these great sages I describe give us the inner strength which inspires us to move ever forward to our own salvation.

Siddha Agastyar is the patron saint of Tamil Nadu and references to him can be found in the literature of both the Southern India's Dravidian Tamil literature and in the Rig Vedic literature of Northern India. Agastyar is also the father of Siddha Medicine that was given to him by the god Shiva. This uses preparations made out of parts of plants and trees such as leaves, bark, stem, roots and so on but may also include minerals and some animal substances. This system of medicine was used in ancient India from before 2000 BC and is believed to be the oldest existing medical system in the world.

There is evidence to suggest that Agastyar was not just a legend but a real historic figure. I have spoken to people who say that he is a Siddha who has – like Babaji – attained a deathless state, has been with us for thousands of years, continues to live to this day and will occasionally reveal himself to help protect Dharma in the Age of Kali Yuga. Today he is said to live near the ashram site in the Tinnevely district at Courtrallam and near Kutralam waterfalls in the Pothigai Mountains of southern Tamil Nadu.

Stories like these flourish in India where, it appears, miracles continue to happen. Occasionally, when talking with local people, I was given hints of incredible stories as mind-boggling as what I'd been told in the Naadi oracles. In one conversation it was mentioned, almost in passing, that Shiva was appearing to people in a nearby jungle area. They told me how he would appear in the form of a dog that could speak and give them spiritual guidance and instructions. All this was accepted by everyone without the slightest skepticism as a self-evident truth. If I visit again, my hosts said they would be pleased to take me to the place to meet Shiva so that I could witness this myself. There were times, in India, when I really felt I had fallen down the rabbit hole and, with so many wondrous stories, may even decide to drop all rationality and just stay there.

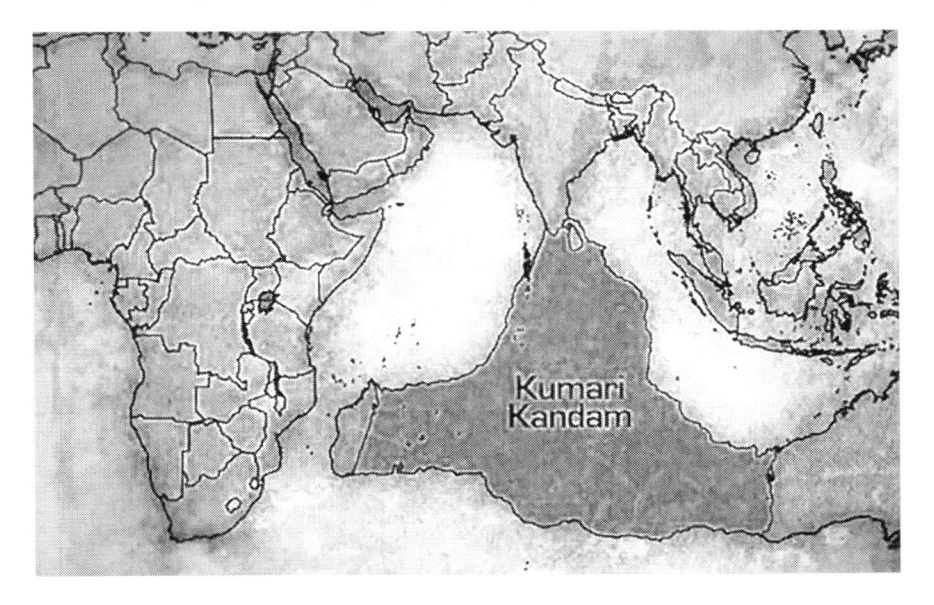

Kumari Kandam

The Siddha yogi's traditions are said to stretch far back into prehistory when India was a sprawling continent that stretched across to join Madagascar to the West and touch Australia in the East. This massive land area is described in the Tamil epics written in the first century A.D. by Ilango Adigal, who called it "Kumari Nadu", but most commonly known today as Kumari Kandam. It is also referenced in the Pandyan legends that tell of lands lost to the ocean, as described in ancient Tamil and Sanskrit literature. European scholars have called this submerged land Lemuria or Gondwanaland.

From 30,000 B.C. to 2,700 B.C. massive earthquakes and shifts of the tectonic plates were gradually sinking the continent from the west until, over thousands of years, all had sunk beneath the ocean.

The people of Kumari Kandam are believed to have been an advanced race with super human powers who migrated, as the floodwaters rose, to populate North and South America, the Nile Valley, Australia and – some say – the continent of Atlantis that lay somewhere in the North Atlantic Ocean. The occultist and theosophist, Madam Helena Blavatsky, claims that she gained knowledge of these people through 'astral clairvoyance'. The populous of Kumari Kandam (She called it Lemuria) she says were the people of what she called the "Third Root Race" – Root races are stages in human evolution. She describes these people as being about 7 feet tall, sexually hermaphroditic, egg-laying, mentally undeveloped and spiritually more pure than the following "Root Races".

According to the archeologist Graham Hancock, who is a proponent of the existence of Kumari Kandam, a discovery made in March 1991 by India's National Institute of Marine Oceanography gives some evidence for the existence of Tamil Kandam: it was the discovery of a 'a horseshoe shaped structure' off-shore of the Tarangambadi-Poompuhar coast near Nagapattinam in Tamil Nadu at a depth of 23 meters and about 5 kms offshore. He speculates that the coastline of Southern India would have submerged about 11,000 years before the present time or 9,000 BC. This makes the discovery of the U-shaped structure 6,000 years older than the oldest civilizations of antiquity. This also ties in with the information given in the celebrated Tamil epic called the "Silappadikaran".

We are talking, here, of archeological theories that are hotly debated and fiercely questioned and some of the ideas of Blavatsky and others are somewhat questionable theories. Nonetheless, it is fascinating to speculate about the strange people of legend who once lived in the times before the deluge in the East and about whether their lost traditions and knowledge persist today in the traditions of the Siddha yogis.

We Reach Brihadeeswarar

It was not until we reached the ancient temple called Brihadeeswarar, located in Thanjur, that Mr. Prakash was able to tell me about what

Maha Ananda Siddha had told him about me when I touched his feet in the ashram. This incredible temple was a fitting place to receive a message from a Siddha yogi as legend says it was a place built using magical powers. This was not a temple that was listed by the Naadi oracles for me to visit and do rituals but it synchronized nicely with everything that was happening. We sat on some steps close to a wall, which was etched in ancient Tamil that Mr. Prakash pointed out was the same sanserif style of Tamil lettering with which the Naadi leaves are written.

He pointed out that the inscriptions on the walls are similar to the Naadi remedies, with daily rituals to be performed for the Linga and with the details of offerings to be made such as jewelry, flowers and textiles and so on. Included are details of the puja to be performed, and at what times. What an amazing place to get such spiritual messages. In the soft evening light this lovely place feels like an ethereal world. Seeing the ancient Tamil inscriptions around us it made me think that the rishis, who wrote the leaves, may have also known places like this.

Brihadeeswarar is over 1,000 years old. They say that this place was impossible to build with the technology of the time. It's all made of granite, the capstone at the top of the temple weighs over 80 tons and legends say the ancients used magical mantras to levitate it into place. Skills that were retained, perhaps, from the lost world of Kumari Kandam?

As we sat on the ancient steps, Mr. Prakash told me about the prophecy Maha Ananda Siddha had made when I touched his feet. He appeared to be angry about something and had told off a young man who had said something derogatory. Afterwards he spoke to Mr. Prakesh about me and told him that in the future I would own properties all over the world and would be doing a great deal of spiritual work for the benefit of mankind. My life would be dedicated entirely to doing spiritual work and I would be known all over the world. This, and other private information, corresponded with what the first Naadi oracle had told me – information that Mr. Prakash knew nothing about. So for me this was a revelation and confirmation of my path ahead. It seemed that India was telling me what to do with my life then reaffirming the information again and again.

It was all a lot to take in. I have already dedicated my life to spiritual work, for this is what my wife Jane and I now do all the time: we are mediums and we give readings to people and I am an exponent of mediumship, demonstrating it and talking about it and writing about it all the time. But now I'm being told to take it to a level that is worldwide and I'm not sure I'm capable of that or if it would ever happen. But who knows what destiny has in store?

When I first consulted the Naadi I thought I was at the end of my journey but it seems the real journey is just beginning. Of course, Maha Ananda Siddha and others could simply be flattering me – except for the fact that this, and other specific things said, had already been told me by the other Naadi readers: things that were unknown to Mr. Prakash.

Noticing that I was moved by what had been said, Mr. Prakash puts his hand on my shoulder and says "God will watch over you at all times".

What a lovely thought.

CHAPTER 11

ॐ

Ramalinga Swamigal

So far on my journey I've tuned into spiritual objects, I've visited ancient temples, met my astrologer guides, climbed a holy mountain, seen the sacred temples, walked a holy pilgrimage and met a holy man who doesn't eat, sleeps in a fire and will live for five hundred years. The 5,000 year old Naadi leaf oracle has told me my past, present and future and now, with my astrologer's advice, I am to change the course of my destiny by performing the various rituals and magic they prescribe as a remedy to my karma.

For the next step in this process we head off on another long drive to the ashram of a Siddha Saint called Ramalinga Swamigal at Mettukuppam, a hamlet near Vadalur. The roads here are worse than ever and, in places, heave with traffic, mopeds, bikes, prams and a sea of humanity. Slamming the car through the commotion, I am amused to see how we are all driving over hot bitumen asphalt that is in the process of being laid directly onto the dusty road. The driver hits the horn and, as we squeal past, we overtake the heavy machinery as it pours tar under us. No sooner is the tarmac laid than it is torn up by the traffic flying by, now with smoking wheels. It seems crazy but, then, this is India.

On route we stop at a village market that's way off the beaten track and buy fruit, flowers and drapery to be used in the ritual of honoring the great Sihha yogi. By doing this ritual, the hope is that we will get the blessing of the saint for the remedy I need to do later which is to feed the children in an orphanage.

Ramalinga Swamigal (also known as Vallalar) was born on October 5, 1823 in the village of Marudur. He is one of the most famous saints of South India but not generally well known to Western spiritual seekers. When he was a toddler his parents took him to the great temple of Dancing Shiva at Chidambaram where the temple head priest ran forward, embraced the laughing boy, and declared that this was a child of God. Ramalinga was able to gain knowledge spontaneously, directly from God, without study. Although he had only 4 years of formal education, he wrote 5,986 songs in his lifetime, many of which are considered to be some of the most beautiful in Indian literature.

His songs and poems focus on the theme that compassion alone is the road to salvation. He tells us that man is black and white but the heart knows no colour and, just as there is only one full moon and one sun for the whole world, so too there is only one God for the entire world. If the heart is damaged then so too is your life damaged but if your heart is powerful then your life will become very powerful. He wanted all beings – animals and humans – to live in harmony. He also felt that the caste system in India was wrong as it caused division. To him all people were equal. All are brothers and sisters.

As I have said already, there are believed to be people in India who are immortal. They are called as chiranjeevi in Hinduism and some gods, such as Hanuman, are said to be physically alive to this day. Their meditation powers do not allow Yama, God of Death, to draw near. The story of Ramalinga Swamigal is another that is hard to believe as he is said to have transcended mortality and become an ever-present being of light. In his stirring discourses he speaks of the 'pure and true' path that he called Sanmargam, to overcome the physical, mental, and spiritual afflictions of humanity. This will lead to Godhood and the ability to conquer death itself.

His philosophy of deathless life he describes as the transformation of the human body until the elixir of life overflows and fills the human body. We are reminded of the deathless yogis like Babaji that I described earlier in this book. Ramalinga Swamigal has predicted that one day this lost knowledge will once again be available to the world, saying "great men of far north will learn this philosophy and come down to preach to you." Could he, perhaps, be referring to the deathless saints of the Himalayas descending to help humanity? There are other Indian prophecies which say that, when the world is near to a point of destroying itself, these great beings will return to teach mankind the lost knowledge of the past and open, again, the paths towards the knowledge of the divine.

The transformation of the corporeal body into the celestial body is not a flight of fancy but a real achievement that Ramalinga publically demonstrated at the end of his life. The process of transformation is initiated by divine rays that make the body translucent – a process that, he says, all of humanity will one day come to understand. We will also learn to attain the deathless state – a secret science that was once known to the Tamil people.

The process of transformation begins with the body becoming resplendent with a golden hue and is transformed into what he calls the Suddha Deham – 'body of love'. After this stage the 'body of love' is transformed again into an effulgent body known as the Pranava Deham – 'body of Grace'. Unlike the previous one this body cannot be sensed by touch as it is a body of light, eventually becoming the Gnana Deham – the 'Body of Wisdom and Bliss'. By following this divine path of Truth and Purity, the most impure body will become a body pure and imperishable. This reminds me a little of the Dzogchen tradition of Tibetan Buddhism that talks about the 'rainbow body' in which the physical body self-liberates into a nonmaterial body of light. However, in the case of Ramalinga Swamigal, this is not some astral process but happens right here on the material plane and for all to see.

Crowds of people witnessed many miracles by Ramalinga. There are reports that he could multiply his physical form and appear at several places at the same time, taking multiple forms of his body at various points in crowded gatherings so that everyone as could see him and hear him speak. He was not against doing miracles, as they form the powers and plays of the Divine. One story of many that I find intriguing was when a magician, hoping to catch him out, requested that he turn mercury into a bead. Ramalinga gently poured the mercury into the hollow of his palm, closed it and on opening the palm revealed the mercury to be a solid bead. On another occasion Ramalinga put a silver rupee coin in his hand and, after a few minutes, it melted into molten silver. The power to do this is called apara marga siddhi.

What I am describing here is reminiscent of the quest of the alchemists to turn base metals into gold. The Swiss psychologist, Carl Jung, interprets in his book *Psychology and Alchemy* (1944) and, in his commentary to the Taoist book *The Secret of the Golden Flower*, saw in alchemy a historic parallel to his own discoveries of the unconscious as well as a symbolic representation of the individuation process – the union of the unconscious with the conscious mind. Ramalinga, however, shows that alchemy is far greater than this comfortable scientific description and is, in fact, a process that transforms not only a person's psychology but also the totality of their being. Ramalinga's alchemy draws on mantra and tantra and, by using herbs, gases and metals, transforms the body into the deathless body. A person who has achieved this state and is completely free of desire could also change base metals into gold. On one occasion he is said to have transmuted sand into golden particles by putting the sand into a vessel of water, which became golden particles that the swami then threw onto the street. On another occasion he was seen to convert an iron sheet into sixteen carat gold by treating it with herbs and then heating it. Ramalinga Swamigal threw away the gold, as someone with this power must have no material attachments, and said: "One who is without desire alone can get this knowledge. Leave off this pursuit of alchemy".

It was also impossible to photograph Ramalinga. His body was so filled with divine light, they said, that nothing would appear on the film. Some devotees brought the famous photographer Masilamani Mudaliar from Madras to the ashram to take a photo of the

Ramalinga. Eight attempts were made to take a picture but every time the skilled photographer failed to get any image on the negative except the white cloth he wore. It is also said that Ramalinga cast no shadow and left no footprints on the ground. When he walked in the pouring rain, everyone with him would get drenched but he'd remain completely dry.

Many miracles surrounded Ramalinga Swamigal's life but the most astonishing occurred on the day of his passing on January 30, 1874. On that day he gave an inspired lecture, entreating his audience to undertake a spiritual quest and look into the "nature of the powers that lie beyond us and move us." He asked his devotees to meditate on the lighted lamp from his room, which he placed outside. He then entered the room, locked himself in, and told his followers not to open the door and that, even if they did dare open it, they would find nothing. His long seclusion triggered many concerns in the ashram and surrounding towns so the Government finally forced the doors open in May of that year. Although the entrance had been guarded day and night by concerned devotees they found nothing. The room was empty, with no clues as to what had happened to Ramalinga Swamigal. He was said to have merged into Light.

It was noon when we arrived at what had once been his ashram. Ramalinga did not believe in the cast system and saw everybody as equals and now, every day, the poor and destitute gather twice a day to be fed with free food. The oven to cook the food has never been extinguished since it was lit by Ramalinga Swamigal on May 23, 1867. He despised money yet was able to provide free vegetarian food to thousands throughout his life and to this day.

We were there as part of my own alchemical inner transformation, and as the prelude to remedies I would do a few days later. As part of clearing my own karma I will soon need to feed the poor. The spiritual energy of Ramalinga – who, like Jesus, had materialized food – would serve as a blessing for my own upcoming ritualistic feeding.

We enter the temple area and pay the priest to perform a personal blessing. Money changes hands but the effect is that the temples have money to feed the poor and do charitable work. In this way, as Sathya Sai Baba says, money comes and goes but virtue comes and grows. Next I get a second blessing by the Sadhu in the nearby shrine near to the door to the room where Ramalinga disappeared. (This is known as Tirukappitta Arai) It was here that Ramalinga resurrected into a light being.

The sadhu in charge takes a special interest in me as our eyes meet. There was a moment of 'connection' and I felt that an energy had been exchanged between us. It is traditional to give pilgrims a small packet of Vibhuti but instead he thrusts dozens of packets into my hands and then leads us to an especially sacred area behind the shrine where westerners and not normally permitted to visit. Mr. Prakesh was beaming as he knew that was very auspicious for the remedies and the charitable feeding I was to do soon.

We are shown around the rest of the Vallalar Temple areas that look strangely like the inside of a Christian church and, as we walk, I am told by a devotee that every year, around the time of his disappearance on the 30th January, crowds of people see Ramalinga Swamigal appear before them as a being of light. The light appears as a spinning ball that emerges from the doors and flashes across the centre of the temple. This is seen by everyone present. As far as I know, there is no documented evidence of this phenomenon, such as photos, but it is nonetheless intriguing to hear that regular miracles continue to take place.

Before my visit to Vallalar Temple I had never heard of Ramalinga Swamigal yet I feel instantly connected with this dead saint. He is said to have never eaten and eventually became a being of light. All strange stuff but what a wonderful goal: not to eat but to make sure everyone else is fed long after you're dead. It's nice to think that we can indirectly share in this as the money given for all these temple blessings and ceremonies helps to put food in hungry bellies.

As we leave, the poor are gathering for the evening meal time. Spotting a few people from earlier in the day, I realize that these guys have been waiting all day. One thing they have that we don't is time. There are facilities here to accommodate hundreds every day.

By now I can really feel the energy surrounding us start to build and I'm sure this must be having a tremendous effect upon my spirit and, with it, my karmic debts. I am definitely buzzing with energy and feel ready to burst. I can feel the energy changing in me as we draw closer to starting the Naadi remedies proper.

On the way out we stop again. What I thought was a public toilet turns out to be another small temple and we go inside to do one last puja. It's getting really late now but we have a few more specific pujas to do before moving on. By now I'd completely lost track of what's next on the remedy list but I have heard that we have a big day tomorrow: a very long drive through the night and a feeding ceremony in the morning. I get my blessing and the gods get my garlands.

Feeding a School

According to the teachings in the Naadi, the three most powerful ways to clear karma and help yourself to spiritually progress is either to plant forest trees, buy someone a cow or feed people. My next prescribed remedy was to feed people and Mr. Prakash had planned this for me. The funds had been sent ahead for the food in advance and all I needed to do now was to turn up and begin the feeding.

The place chosen was the 'Challenged Children Women and Education Trust' (C.C.W.E Trust) located in Chidambaram, Tamil Nadu, India. It is a school for 83 mentally challenged children, aged from 5 to 14, as well as some orphans and a few old people. With very limited means and budgets, the children are "given stimulation and education to help them to live independently. The vocational training includes making envelopes, greeting cards, chalks, candles, tailoring work and craft work." They are given medical and psychological help together with physiotherapy. The therapies also include yoga, dance, music, drawing, sports and physical training.

All of the above sounds very accomplished but I could see, as I walked up the steps, that the reality is that this place runs on love not money. This was clearly a desperately poor organization, which was doing great work with very limited means.

To my left, as I entered the building, I could see battered and well-loved toys and little cages with birds that were clearly the backbone of the schools resources. "Hurry, hurry," says Mr. Prakesh 'They are ready to eat now."

Before me I see lines of well-behaved children sitting on the floor in four long lines with banana leaves in front of them. I am given a big pot of food and, after they chant a prayer, I serve every child by hand. I put the rice on the leaves and, behind me, the other carers put an assortment of vegetables, pickles, papadum and other condiments on the leaves. Everyone eats with their hands. The banana leaf acts as a disposable plate and itself is not consumed. Mr. Prakesh had made sure, also, that the food we supplied was of the very best quality and you could see the children's eyes light up as the delicious food was put on their leaves. Afterwards, everyone folds their leaf inwards as a sign of gratitude to the host, and says together in a loud voice 'Nanri!' – Thank you.

It was lovely to feed children but I could also feel something happening to me on an energetic level. Firstly it was very emotional to be so close to seriously deprived children, and to see the light in their eyes was deeply moving. But also all this spiritual merit and energy, accumulated from visiting the Ramalinga Swamigal temples and the Arunachala mountain, seemed to fire up inside me. Something was happening to me that was far more than the eye could see. On a deep level in the very heart of my soul something was changing. A release was taking place and a flower of compassion was starting to bloom. I now understood that what I was doing was filled with grace and is a glorious magical act of personal transformation.

Doing this makes me think of Jane back home. For seven years she was a SRN psychiatric nurse for children and did lots of work helping desperately challenged children. It's kind of a strange coincidence that I should be told to do a little of the same. Maybe

Jane had cleared some of her karma by doing similar acts. I think of my own children and grandchildren and what lessons we can learn from the shining eyes of these less fortunate kids.

As we leave, my emotions turn to a feeling of mild anger. How I'd love it if there were more people in my profession (astrologers, psychics and mediums) who could be less concerned about money and kudos and instead use some of the proceeds from their spiritual work to help people. Similarly my thoughts turned to the disgraceful way modern charities waste money on fat cat wages and massively expensive marketing campaigns. I had recently read that one in five of the UK's biggest charities are spending less than half of their income on good causes and that, in some of the worst cases, only one percent actually gets to the people in need. It seems that all we are feeding are charity machines, which are often driven by obscene overheads and salaries, aggressive fundraising, and bloated marketing and publicity departments. If we eat in front of the TV they drive home messages of starvation and global poverty and try to make us pay up because of guilty feelings rather than from love. This drowns the very joy of charity and negates the blessing that giving with love brings to both the recipient and the giver. How far this corporate world takes us from the lovely feeling here that simply makes me want to give more and more until my pockets are empty.

It was also becoming clear as to why the Naadi had urged me, in the readings, to set up a charitable foundation to build spiritual centres and do work like this. I would make a start as soon as I got home. Perhaps there's a way I can bring others to India to feed people in this spiritual way so that they, too, can know the joy of inner transformation that comes from putting food directly onto the plates of the hungry.

CHAPTER 12

ॐ

Strange Remedies & Rituals

Some people think that, to do the remedies, you have to convert to Hinduism or forsake your own religious beliefs but this is not the case as Hinduism, unlike many major religions, does not adhere to any strict concept of orthodoxy. You can participate in Hindu rituals and ceremonies, without fear of feeling awkward, simply by having a willingness to understand its beliefs and engage in its practices. A Hindu needs only to have a simple desire and commitment to study the scriptures and follow the proper practices. When Jane and I have been to temples in the UK we felt a little awkward at first as we didn't want to offend through ignorance of the correct observances, or feel that we were gate-crashing holy places. We were made very welcome and no one thought twice about seeing a white face in a predominantly Indian community. There's no hard-sell to join up, pressure to convert, give donations or anything like that. You just join in and enjoy the pageant and community spirit. It is not exclusive in the sense that one must be formally recognized in order to be a practitioner.

There is a minority of conservative Hindus who consider it to be a birthright and that, if you are not born a Hindu, you can never become one but this is a dated and misguided position that few Hindus hold to be true. The priests I met looked to the person standing before them and, in some cases when our eyes met, they would invite me and my group into areas of the temples that were not open to everyone. They could tell that we were on a special pilgrimage and in search of higher truth.

Part of my remedies is to do puja – ritual worship – to the various gods prescribed in my Naadi leaves. I had already done some of these in the UK and have described what happened, in my first book about the Naadis. Puja can be performed at home, as part of your individual spiritual work, or in temples. They involve ritual actions such as cleansing idols representing Hindu deities, making offerings and chanting of spiritual scriptures. Most of the sophisticated Puja and fire rituals I needed to do, collectively identified as a yajna, would be done by a holy man/priest on my behalf. All I needed to do is sit on the floor, as the Puja takes place, and tune in to the energy of the proceedings.

Puja is done to connect with the power of God (Brahman – the single binding unity behind the diversity) that manifests in the many forms of the Hindu pantheon of gods and deities. If we make this connection then, through the ritual, we can clear some of our karma to allow our life to grow to its full potential and eventually to allow us to become freed from Samsara. (The cycle of death and rebirth to which life in the material world is bound.)

Ayushya Homam

As part of the remedies it was arranged for me to perform a fire ceremony called a Homam. This would be done at a small temple that we'd hired for the day together with a group of priests who would chant the mantras and guide me through my part in the ceremony. I have already explained that we westerners can sometimes find it a little awkward doing puja as the ornate Hindu ceremonies and pantheon of gods, despite our intellectual acceptance, can feel very far removed from the culture we are used to.

To take part in the ceremony I am to wear new clothes, which we'd bought earlier in the market. For the temple ritual I was to dress like a holy man, which included wearing a lungi wrapped around my waist, Mala beads around my neck and a rudraksha seed wristband. Around my head I wear an ornate piece of yellow, green and gold cloth printed with Sanskrit chats, which is tied around my head with a big knot in the centre. As is the tradition in a temple, men do not cover their upper body so I could now proudly reveal all my flab to Simon's camera the world at large. I have to admit I felt a little awkward on one level – particularly as, later when driving back, I spotted a group of young girls burst into astonished snickers to see a white man dressed like this – but I was nonetheless up for it. I did look odd but I could either resist and spoil the whole thing or jump in with both feet. I chose the latter option.

A Homam is an ancient fire ritual that is sometimes called a homa or havan or yajna (yagya) or yajana. The Homam is an ancient tantric ritual where oblation or any religious offering is made into fire.

Homams are an elaborate form of Puja that are performed for a particular deity by invoking Agni, the god of fire. Agni is considered to be the mouth of the gods and goddesses, and the medium who conveys offerings to them. Similarly, the Sun is considered to be the main source of energy, and fire is seen as a representation of the Sun's energy. An offering to the fire god is also an offering to the Sun.

Throughout, I was acutely aware of how all this takes us far back into the past and to the rituals of the archaic men and even to pre-Homo Sapiens times. The whole idea of doing a fire ritual evoked in me a sense of connection with these first humans who must have gazed upon fire and seen it as incomprehensible holy, something of awe and wonder. Like a god, the fire could provide light, warm us, cook food, protect us from dangerous animals and even transform some stones into metal. As we look into the fire, and surrender ourselves, we step into this same primordial world; a world of irrational forces retained in the residual memories of our unconscious. In the images that leap forth from the flames we see reflections of ourselves and pointers to the path of our own inner transformation.

A Homam is done in Hindu temples to enrich energy or to destroy any undesirable quality in the environment. There are many types of Homam: mine is to be an Ayushya Homam, which is dedicated to the Ayur Devatha – the Life God – to enhance longevity and good health. (The word *Ayusha* means 'age'.) It is said that even ailments, which cannot be diagnosed through mainstream medicines or have not yet arisen in the body yet, are cured by the performance of this Homam. It will also get rid of any obstacles on one's life path.

A special fire altar had been made out of bricks on the floor of the temple and arranged into a mandala. The bricks had the three lines of Shiva marked on them using ash. Near this was a long table that was covered in fruits to be used as part of the offering. A great deal of preparation has gone into this ceremony and we have gathered together many special herbs from all over India. Everything here has been specially put together for the ceremony and will be dismantled afterwards.

After making chants and puja to the god Ganesh by putting fruit in front of a Kalash (large copper pot) filled with water and coconut water, I am given a place to sit by the fire altar and my finger is tied as a symbol of being connected to the benevolent powers from the gods. It's a bit like the tying of the knot from a pre-Christian wedding ceremony. I'm told then to bang my temples – I never did find out why I had to do this; maybe it symbolizes an awakening of some kind? Another mantra is recited and offerings are made of water, Chandan (sandalwood) paste, Sindoor (vermilion), rice, milk mixed with floral-scented oil, flowers, fruits and sweets.

Next, I have to call out my name, mother's name, father's name, wife's name and so on. The priest repeats it and the fire ceremony itself can start. It strikes me that the names and their order are exactly the same as the details that were written in the Naadi leaves when I first consulted them. The Naadi oracle had known this same information thousands of years ago. It had all been written on the leaves and now here I was, thousands of years later, calling it out. I had an eerie feeling that the rishis were somehow looking into this moment, their celestial eyes gazing across the millennia and far into the future as they wrote the leaves about me. Many strange things run through my mind as we chant to invoke the gods and I open myself to the hypnotic power of the rituals.

One of the priests makes fragrant flower offerings to the gods while another prepares the small baskets of 108 different aromatic and medicinal herbs gathered from all over India. Sandalwood, small pieces of Banyan tree, fragrant herbs and pure ghee are used as an offering to the Agni. I am handed a basket of fruit and told to walk with it, clockwise around the temple. The fruit is put into the consecrated fires that now burn with a fury as ghee is poured into them. All this is to help me to clear my past and to ward off evil influences in the future. Like the phoenix, the spirit is reborn. As the fire burns so does my karmic debt.

As mantras are chanted and the temple fills with smoke, I am to empty the 108 baskets of herbs, one by one into the flames, on the cue of the priest. Every time the mantras come to the word 'svaha' – which means "so be it" and is said at the end of a mantra just as a Christian may say "Amen".

Some of the herbs, which I am placing in the fire, are said to transmit medicinal smoke that cures lots of diseases. Many of these herbs are very rare indeed and found only in obscure areas of the Himalayas. From the black residue in the embers of the fire, the priests will make a paste that I can keep and use in times of need. When I'm given it after all the proceedings I am told that, if I place a small dot of this residue between my eyebrows at important times such as a business meetings and so on, it will serve to protect me and give me the power to win the day. It must never be worn at funerals or, in my specific case, when I'm doing mediumship.

To be sitting so close to the fire to do the Ayushya Homam is, of course, suffocatingly hot work in the Indian climate. I knew a little bit about Ayushya Homam from my studies but was blissfully unaware of the final stage. Lost in thought about how Prometheus stole the fires from the gods of Greece, I am thinking that the ceremony is coming to a close when I'm told we must now go into the temple courtyard and I am to kneel down and close my eyes.

"Now you have bath,' says Mr. Prakash. Clearly I must have misunderstood him again. Bath? I don't like the sound of that, I think as I kneel on the cold floor with my eyes closed. He must mean when we find a hotel.

I am taken completely by surprise as they now, unexpectedly, pour a Kalash (large pot) of ice cold water and coconut water all over me. It was like being pulled out of a furnace, slapped around the face with a dead fish and then thrown headfirst into the Artic Sea! I'm choking for breath as I fight back my laughter and exasperation. Talk about an Ice Bucket Challenge! Fortunately, Simon caught it all on camera and I hadn't expelled any expletives. Our producer, Louis Frost, back home in England and waiting to do the edit, would love this footage but little of what could be seen comes any way near to describing the momentous feelings of change and transformation that were happening in the unseen world within me.

Abhishekam

With the conclusion of the Ayushya Homam fire ceremonies I now have to lay prostrate on the floor as we conclude with a ceremony called Abhishekam, which is a sacred bath of milk given to a deity. It's a symbol, not so much of cleaning the god, but of cleaning yourself. Milk is, of course, also a potent symbol. It is from the mother's milk that we grow from baby to child and it is a symbol of wholesomeness and the protection of the mother. We pour copious quantities of milk over the temple's Shiva Linga – this ceremony is called Panchamrit Abhishekam of Lord Shiva and is said to bring great good luck and prosperity to the material and spiritual lives of the participants.

Some of these ceremonies took me by surprise but I did feel that something was also happening on an energetic level. Call it psychological, if you like, but I felt something going on in the very depths of my being. Something that is really impossible to describe unless you've opened yourself to these things.

Let's buy a cow

If we understand the fact that everything is Brahman (God), including ourselves, then every word we say, every action we make and every thought and feeling we have for good and bad, will resonate in the heart of Brahman. If we do a good action with sincerity, devotion and a pure heart for someone in desperate need, then the vibrations from this act will resonate through the Universe. So powerful is this energy that it transmutes the influences arising from the past to bring positive things in the future.

One of the most important remedies shown in my Naadi is to do a 'cow and calf donation to a poor female'. This would help to clear the negative effects of past life karma and facilitate some of the positive prophecies found in my Brahma Sukshma Naadi. Mr. Prakash made all the arrangements and a cow and calf would be purchased for me to sign over to a poor woman. The first step was a series of smoky rituals at Mr. Prakash's offices, where I pay homage to these incredible leaves that have been transcribed down through the centuries and hold the secrets of my past life, my present life and my destiny. We give fruit offerings to the leaves themselves and to the great Maharishis, whose incredible clairvoyance made all of this possible.

It seemed like a surreal thing to be doing as we came to the village where the donation would be completed. Waiting for us was the man who had the cow and calf for sale. He had been selected, as it was known to Mr. Prakash that this man had many financial difficulties and that this sale would make a huge difference to his life. Standing nearby was a tiny old lady and her husband who would be receiving the cow.

It's not often we city folk buy cows. Surprisingly, it involves quite a lot of contractual paperwork that Mr. Prakash had organized though a lawyer. For a few minutes I owned a cow and calf and, once all the documentation was complete, I could now legally give the animals to the lady and her husband. I was handed the rope tether and led the cow and calf toward the couple. It was a strange thing but, when I caught the eye of the cow, it was as if it somehow knew that something special was going on. I was getting flashes of Krishna going across my mind and a feeling of huge energy building up inside me. I was becoming aware of the scale of what I was doing with this remedy. Not only was I about to help someone but I could feel the resonance of these actions stretching into my previous lives and into this life. It felt that I too was about to be untethered.

In India the old and the destitute have no big pensions or welfare but if they own a cow they are set up for life as it provides milk, fuel and a guaranteed income. Buying a cow at a good price from someone in debt can also free them from problems, too. Also, if you directly do someone a good turn they will often think good thoughts about you. We spiritualists believe that thoughts are things so these positive thoughts will uplift the giver and also help to break their karmic bonds.

When I handed the rope tether to the old lady I felt overwhelmed with emotion. Perhaps it was the result of all the rituals beforehand; perhaps it was because I was tired; perhaps it was because her eyes showed such gratitude but something inside me seemed to snap. My heart pounded and I felt so honored to be in a position to do something so humbling and lovely. Giving to charity is one thing but physically to place a life-changing thing in a person's hand is a deeply moving experience.

Clearly there were energetic and karmic changes happening but deep, deep down in my soul I could truly feel the greatest knowledge of all: that everything is Brahman, everything is Love.

CHAPTER 13

Mysterious Temples

Mystic Journeys tend not to be in straight lines. The Naadi leaves had given a list of Puja that I was to perform in temples across Southern India and the logical thing to do would be to have visited them in a nice orderly sequence on a well-planned route. But this did not take into account the positions of the planets and the auspicious days when the Puja could be performed. For example Puja to Shiva are best performed on a Monday and Puja to the planet Mercury need to be performed on a Wednesday so, even if the temples are right next to one another, the Puja cannot be performed at the same time. The Naadis had also named specific temples for the Puja so the result was that we zigzagged all over Southern India to do the right Puja at the right place and at the right time when the planets were in the perfect positions.

I lost count of how many temples we visited but we estimated that we did over 2,000 miles of travel all crammed into the three weeks we'd allowed for the trip. And, of course, the thick Indian dialects and hard to pronounce town names made it all so confusing that Simon and I often had no idea where we were or whether we were about to travel for a few hours or a few days. To this day I still don't know the location of many of the holy places we went to so I cannot include them here and, if I did, it would make my narrative a bit dry. This book is not a travelogue about India, it's about the inner journey we all make and specifically what happens when we start to unstitch our karma through a spiritual pilgrimage. What follows next is some of the most interesting highlights about the holy places, pageants and rituals I had to do. I hope it may whet your appetite and inspire you, perhaps, to take your own inner – or outer – spiritual journey.

Ramanathaswamy Temple

Ramanathaswamy Temple is a Hindu Temple, dedicated to the god Shiva, located on Rameswaram island in the eastern shore of the state of Tamil Nadu. It was the place identified in my first Naadi readings where I was to go to do Puja to Shiva. We'd travelled through the day and into the night to get to our 'Government Hotel' at about 2:00 am. I was so desperately tired from the days and nights of travel that I collapsed onto the bed to grab a few hours' sleep and be ready for an early start the next day.

The sheets stank, the air conditioning didn't work, the shower wouldn't switch off properly and the room was filthy and furnished with strange Bakelite ornaments and garish lamp shades that looked as if they'd come out of a jumble sale from the 1950's. Did I care?

"And to think this is the best room in the hotel," I chuckled to myself, "the Bridal Suite, the man had said. Those poor brides."

I sank into the disgusting bed, gagging slightly at the rancid smell, and flipped into an instant deep sleep as the bugs feasted on my pink flesh, rats looked on and the heavy fan flopped and wobbled on the ceiling.

I dressed, as instructed by Mr. Prakash, in my traditional Indian sarong – made from an orange cotton sheet wound around my waist like a towel. We met at 5:00 am on the veranda to begin the first stage of the day's remedies, which was sit in meditation and watch the sun rise over the sea. This was a symbolic act that would represent the rebirth of the soul.

I expected that the viewpoint we found by the sea would be isolated but, as the sun broke, dozens of people joined us to watch the incredible display as the cadmium yellow light slowly spread across the horizon. There is something deeply spiritually special about India. The official name of India is Bharat, which itself comes from the name of a god of fire and light – like the sun itself. Where else in the world would so many people gather every morning at a viewpoint like this one, simply to watch the sun rise?

I was beginning, now, to really feel the spirit of India seeping into my soul and causing huge inner changes. I could sense a new light dawning within me. Despite the residue of tiredness, I was beginning to feel more and more focused and, as I watched the sun, contemplated the idea that whatever happens out there – in the world

– is a reflection of, and maybe even caused by, what's happening in here – inside me. The nature of the self is like light. It is joyful and happy. Once we are focused on the inner light we need travel no further for we have found an unshakable happiness that nothing can harm. Need we ever move from this present moment? The past is gone. The future, it seems, is already set and may already have happened. But the present moment is God's gift and is there forever.

As I wait, ready to set off to do my next series of rituals and remedies, dawn brings to mind notions of illumination and hope, with a chance for happiness and improvement.

The next remedy I have to do at Ramanathaswamy Temple is to wash away the negative karma from my past lives. I have been travelling India to do a series of spiritual remedies that the Naadi Astrologers have said is the result of my former life as an Indian Rishi. The rituals dictate that my first step today must be into the sea.

The astrologers next drive me to a spot close to the temple at Agni Tirtha where I am to bath in the sea. This is a Puja called "Samudra Snanam" which is to prepare me for the "Teerth Snanam" that will be performed in the temples. I know all these words now but, at the time, I had no idea what to expect. Samudram means Sea (literally the "gathering together of waters"), while Snanam means bathing, and this act is done before entering the temple itself that is situated 300 meters from the shoreline. Here the water is peaceful and shallow without any tides at all. These are the sacred waters of the Agniteertham that legend says were calmed by Rama. Sea water – just like the holy rivers of India – has a special quality and here, I was told, three different types of sea water vibrations converge. The beach itself is covered in litter and flotsam but I take a dip in the water as prescribed by the Naadi.

The next Puja – "Teerth Snanam" – is to be performed in the temple. The words mean 'Holy Bath' but, with the impossible to understand accents, Simon and I just nodded as if we understood and just accepted we'd run with whatever happens.

"I think it's something to do with dentistry," says Simon.

Ramanathaswamy Temple is an awe-inspiring building. Built by different rulers of Chola Dynasty in the 12th century, it is a fine example of Dravidian architecture. It was a king of Sri Lanka who, according to inscriptions, built the sanctum of the temple.

We approached it barefoot as we left the sea shore and it rose above us like a brilliant yellow mountain. The temple is shaped like a conch and this tower is 38.4 meters high. Inside, it is renowned for its magnificent prakaras or corridors with massive sculptured pillars on each side.

To the amazement of Mr.Prakash, we walked straight into the temple without anyone before us. Normally, and particularly at festival times, there are huge queues but there was nobody in line. We walked straight in. Mr. Prakash took this as a very auspicious sign. He couldn't believe that, once again, the temples just opened up to us as if they were welcoming us with a personal invitation.

We were hastened though some dark corridors where fire ceremonies were happening. The place was thick with smoke and incense, and the black rock walls and pillars rose ominously out of the fuming smokes; flashes of the lights from bright orange fires danced off the carved walls. We did a Puja with a priest in front of a shrine to Shiva in the inner section of the temple that is not usually open to non-Hindus and next entered the first of the places where water is drawn. Here began the first of the Teerth Snanam.

As we go through to the main areas we turn a corner to be greeted by a painted elephant that is trained to accept donations. I put some rupee notes in my hand and the elephant takes them with his trunk and puts them neatly in the donation bowl. He then raises his trunk and, in a magical surreal moment, taps me on the head three times as a blessing to the pilgrim. (Sadly, I read later that these elephants are not well treated, which takes the shine off things a little.)

"Now you have bath, bath!" said Mr. Prakash as he waved us forward to the priest. "Bath, bath, bath. Come on for bath, sir".

It's a little disconcerting when you enter a temple to be suddenly told it's time for a bath. Fortunately these happen fully clothed as water is drawn from a well and a little from a ladle is poured over the worshiper. Unbeknown to me, Mr. Prakash had arranged for me to have a 'super-size-me' deal in which full buckets of water are poured over me at each well. The temple has 22 wells that are said to contain holy water with different spiritual qualities. These are not all usually open to non-Hindus but permission had been given for me to enter all parts of the temple. Sadly we could not get permission to film any of the events but this is understandable considering the sacredness of this site.

It was great fun as well as being an inspiring symbolic act. This is a full-on cleansing of the soul that leaves you shivering and shaking with delight. Legend has it that Lord Rama himself is said to have bathed here.

The 22 wells (Theerthams) of the temple all taste different and are said to give different blessings. Beside each one is a sign in English that names the wells and their qualities. For example, the first well is called the Mahalakshmi Theertham and is on the South of the Hanuman Temple, where Dharmarajan bathed and became rich. This cascade of well water brings financial good fortune to the person blessed here. Every well has a different legend and blessing associated with it for things such as getting rid of curses, purification of the heart, removing poverty, protection from Hell, attaining wisdom and so on.

"Close your eyes and pray for your family, sir," says Mr. Prakash as water tumbles over me. With each drenching I focused on the qualities of the well and visualized cleansing and renewal. One that particularly interested me was the Chandra Theertham in the inner corridors of the temple that gives the knowledge of the past, present and the future and enables the aspirant to reach the worlds they want. Another offered the powers of clairvoyance and mediumship.

Naturally some will say that this is a load of silly superstition and throwing well water over someone will not do anything to help them progress spiritually or in any other way. This was not the feeling I had. By now I was completely immersed in India and I did genuinely experience a tremendous feeling of change and transformation. Supporting me throughout was the thought of the amazing empirical facts that the Naadi had told me through the oracles and, now, here I was performing the very rituals and puja that the Rishis had prescribed for me thousands of years ago. Once you connect in this way then, I believe, incredible things can be done within ourselves that will eventually change the external world around us too. God cannot be tricked by rituals but, if our heart is engaged in the process, then anything is possible.

Afterwards we were given permission to film my reactions to all that had just happened. When I look at this footage now I am a little shocked at how tired I look. My face looks drawn but my eyes have a light in them, which shows that something very significant and profound has just happened to my soul. We filmed in the magnificently ornate, huge and awe-inducing corridors that are the longest in the world and held by some 1,212 pillars, each of them measuring 30 feet in height, with most having compositions carved on them. Through the tall corridors echoed the chants of the trainee priests (Pujari) that we had passed on our way through the temple complex. The temple guardian priest allowed us to do one take in this incredible setting.

I'm not normally lost for words but I could hardly speak as all of this had had such a deep and profound effect on me. Remember that we were not here sightseeing or even there to make a movie; we were there, first-and-foremost, to do the remedies and if we could catch some or most of it on camera then that was good. Simon had to dash behind me and sometimes just hope for the best and pray that he could capture the action on camera. There was not much opportunity for planning and direction; we just had to grab footage as things happened and, most of the time, we had no idea where we were or where we'd be next! On a spiritual and vibration level things were happening to a very well planned order, set, perhaps, by the rishis all those thousands of years ago when they prescribed my remedies. The spiritual energy which all this was building inside me was getting to the point that I now felt I wanted to burst.

I know that our producer – Louis Frost – sitting back in rainy England, would be disappointed that we'd not been able to film all these visually stunning and fast moving sequences. And the elephant! So many things missed that he'd emphasized on his production checklist: "Elephants, elephants, elephants – make sure you get me some footage of elephants," he had said before we left. "You can't show India without elephants!"

Looks as if we'd missed the lot but what an incredible inner experience to take home in my heart.

Our journey over the following days took us to the Vivekananda Rock Memorial, which is a popular tourist monument in Vavathurai, and an important place to me as I have been very inspired by the teacher Vivekananda and mentioned him on a number of occasions in my other books. It was at this place that Swami Vivekananda is said to have attained enlightenment and here we were able to rest awhile and meditate in the island's meditation hall.

Wherever we went we visited temples to complete the many pujas that had accumulated through my previous Naadi readings, which I'd had in the past. One place, which Mr. Prakash considered most important to visit, was the Christian Basilica at Velankanni that lies on the Coromandel Coast of the Bay of Bengal. The town is home to a significant Roman Catholic Latin Rite shrine, called the *Basilica of Our Lady of Good Health*, where Mr. Prakash suggests I light a candle. It is interesting how the Naadi remedies have asked me also to take in a Christian site as well as Hindu temples. This is in preparation for my next charitable work that will be part of the remedies but, before visiting more holy places and being thrown into more rituals, we take a stroll on the nearby beach.

The *Basilica of Our Lady of Good Health* is considered sacred by both Christians and Hindu because of the miracle that happened when this area was badly hit by the Tsunami on December 26th 2004. People were bathing happily, like the people I saw as we walked along the beach, when the sea sank back and then stampeded onto the shore, drowning thousands. The sea enveloped the beach and flooded the nearby streets that we drove along to get to the church. The furious sea had burst through the town and didn't stop until it reached the church gate. The locals considered this to be a miracle, which added to other miracles that had happened at this same spot, including the apparition of Mary and the Christ Child to a slumbering shepherd boy, the curing of a lame buttermilk vendor, and the rescue of Portuguese sailors from a violent sea storm. The sudden stopping of the Tsunami served to reinforce these local legends.

Lighting a candle at this bleached white Basilica felt like a good addition to all the Hindu based rituals that I'd already completed. When you think about it, all religions are much the same at heart. Their messages are about love and service to others. And they all believe in the One God – a God that is omnipresent – that is everywhere at the same time. And, just like the gods of India, the One God can take many forms and the universal truths are expressed through divinely charged saints, teachers, avatars, prophets and messiahs. It strikes me that they are all saying the same thing.

I'd seen a lot of charitable acts whilst in India. I'd noticed that some of the poorest people I met were the most generous of all and were only too keen to share the little they had with me. Now it's my turn as, after the visit to the Basilica, I'm to do another of the prescribed remedies, which is to feed some poor villagers. A few days before, we'd stopped at a similar village in the middle of the night and were swarmed by people wanting to look at us – in the near pitch dark we were pulled out of the car so that we could shake hands with the lord mayor. (We'll that's how Simon and I understood it.)

When you feed a stranger it is a powerful medicine, for not only do you help them, but their positive thoughts towards you help your own spirit to flower. It's an antidote to bad karma. The driver stopped by a main road in the countryside and we walked down the mud track towards the small village of grass roofed houses. When they see Simon and me laden with baskets of fruit the whole village turns out. Soon we are surrounded by expectant faces with bright white eyes hoping to share in our sweet produce.

By western standards the fruit we distributed did not cost a great deal but this was clearly a boon to these desperately poor villagers. Their eyes would light up when one gave them a gift and some of the children's faces beamed as if it were Christmas morning. I was struck by just how much can be achieved with just a little money and again how good it feels to put food directly into the hands of the needy. Some of the little children cried at me in terror and Mr. Prakash, noticing my concern, touched my shoulder and said 'It's okay, it's okay, these boys have never seen a white face before. It scares them!'

CHAPTER 14

ॐ

Mystic Mangroves

When all the remedies were done, we took some time out to visit the mangrove forest at Pichavaram, near Chidambaram, which is the world's second largest mangrove forest and somewhere I could reflect on everything that had happened. It also gave Simon the opportunity to film some beautiful scenery. "Incredible footage," he gasps; "So beautiful... Louis is going to work wonders with this. Cannes here we come!"

We get into a boat and are carefully checked to ensure we are wearing a life jacket that everyone in all the boats promptly removes the instant we are out of sight of the boathouse watchtower. We float past lush emerald green trees threading their black roots through the shallow waters and see strange bright coloured birds darting through the foliage. We pass young fishermen lifting their nets, heavy with fish, from the muddy still waters.

Once we are deep into the forest, some of the Indians on an accompanying boat shout with excitement to see a rare water dog otter splash through the water and scuffle through the undergrowth beside us, too fast to catch on camera.

As we were rowed, and sometimes quietly drifted, through the mangroves that spread out for 1100 hectares in a maze of estuaries, I had time to contemplate all that had happened.

So what's all this been about so far? There were some pretty far out predictions made by the oracle that brought me here to India and triggered all of these amazing adventures. The oracle tells me that, once the remedies are done, then there's a great deal of spiritual work ahead for my wife Jane and me. We've been working very hard with our mediumship over the years but it says that, in the future, we will be able to do our work for free. This will be achieved, it said, by setting up a charitable trust – a foundation – so that we can travel and do our work and open centres around the world. Could this be true? Now as I write, nearly a year after these events, I'm pleased to know that the predicted events have started to unfold and money has been given to us already to make a start with these grandiose spiritual plans – not enough to buy a centre, by any means, but I'm inspired by the generosity of ordinary people who have helped.

This mystical journey has certainly changed me and my perspective on life. I'd learnt from India that earthly life is the place we come to work out our karma. To have had such an opportunity to do this quickly, with the guidance of the Siddha yogis/Maharishis through the Naadi, was a gift greater than winning the lottery. The opportunity to become free of karma is a chance for the soul to ascend to the highest levels of awareness. I understand, now, why they say that even celestial beings yearn to take human birth.

It is the work of holy people to awaken people and free them from the cycle of birth and death. Perhaps it was not God's original plan to have beings endlessly spin on a wheel of illusion. Human life may have been a temporary plan in the great scheme: earthly life was there to help us awaken but, somehow, we became attached to material things and forgot the reason we came here.

India, for me, was an awakening for it showed me how we can

become free of the bondage of karma through magical ritual and by doing charitable acts and how, ultimately, these processes can free us completely from the bondage of the ego. When you understand that, really, it's all God unfolding then you realize that even our will is in the hands of the divine. To know this is forever to be drawn by the benevolent currents of God's plan. And soon the cosmic plan will lead me back to my familiar life in England and all these things will become a memory, of an experience now gone, that maybe I'll write about some day.

Every experience becomes a memory and even the memories fade in time leaving just an echo that resonates into our future. The ancient mangrove forest seems to project a mild mood of melancholy as I think about how the river of time moves on through this life and into future lives. The words of the great composer, Gustave Mahler, come to mind when he made a comment about reincarnation: "We all return. It is this certainty that gives meaning to life, and it does not make the slightest difference whether or not, in a later incarnation, we remember the former life. What counts is not the individual and his comfort, but the great aspirations to the perfect and the pure, which goes on in each incarnation."

Before leaving for my flight home I had to pay Mr. Prakash for my remedies, car rental and the hire of the temple for the fire ceremony etc. He did not have a card payment facility, which meant I'd taken cash with me and, throughout our adventures, had a large roll of rupees rolled up in my pocket – which is not the best of ideas when travelling abroad. When I'd left England I'd been searching for ages to find suitable trousers with a strong, secure, zipped pocket and, throughout the Indian journey, I was constantly worrying and checking that my huge roll of rupees was safe. I looked like a man who needed a penis reduction op. I'd had a few unexpected expenses and dipped into the money, so now needed to use a cash point machine.

The cash point was in a tatty booth with two ancient looking cash machines but, as there was a very long queue, everyone crammed inside, standing shoulder to shoulder and leaning on one another to edge their way to the front. I put one hand on my zipped pocket just in case of pick pockets.

The booth was a seething oven of sweat, steamy glass and peeling paint and people trod on one another's toes as the slow process of getting to the cash machine unfolded. Eventually I shuffled to the front of the queue and put in my card. Pushed hard against the machine by the crowd, I entered the amount and my pin number. Despite selecting English a card rejected message popped up on the screen in Tamil. "Give me the card; I'll try for you sir," says Mr. Prakash. "What is your PIN number?" I whisper to Gopie "Tell him it's 6384".

"It's 6384!!" Gopie shouts across the jammed room of impatient hot people all struggling to get to my machine. "Okay got it, 6-3-8-4", he repeats slowly. The screen flickers a few times and dies. Mr. Prakash bangs the cash machine but nothing happens. A man behind offers to help and starts banging the machine, too, as does another but still we get problems. A stranger takes my card "Here let me try. What's the PIN number?" Gopie obliges with the number again but, despite entering numbers and yet more banging by random participants, nothing happens. Another man steps forward. "Let me try sir. What's the PIN number?"

"It won't work. Use the other machine," says Mr. Prakash to Gopie who by now had pressed his way in front of the second machine. "Pass me the card", he shouts across the room. A surly looking turbaned ruffian takes my card that is passed from one person to another across the sardine tight crowd. "What's the PIN number again?" "6384" groan the crowd in unison. After three or four tries the machine eventually spits out the money, which, together with my card, is passed between strangers and across the room to me.

It felt that half of India now knew my PIN number and had handled my money. Fortunately not a rupee went missing and, although I didn't get a chance to change my PIN until I got home, my card wasn't compromised. To think how much I'd panicked before and during the journey to watch my money. I think there was a bit of what they call a Leela at work here – a cosmic joke, the sport of Brahman.

"Did you bring me a nice spiritual gift, besides just your washing, back from India? My iron has been missing you," quipped Jane as I arrive home bedraggled and stinking of sewers. I fumbled through my rucksack and handed her the amazing ruby ring that I'd bought her from the shop where I'd done the psychometry.

"How about this?' I say as I hand her the beautiful ruby ring. "Is madam happy?' I say in an Indian accent and moving my head from side to side as they do.

"Very happy," she replies. "Very happy."

Jane was delighted, of course, particularly after so long without my wonderful presence and the housekeeping opportunities I provide.

Maybe she'll let me go again?

CHAPTER 15

ॐ

Physical Mediumship

On my return from India I felt inspired to re-look at my spiritual life and see if there were ways I could take my work as a medium to a new level. I wanted to make all these wonderful experiences part of my work and become a good example to other sincere mediums who were trying to walk on the true spiritual path. In India I had seen incredible things and was inspired by how many people worked for free and were devoted to their gods, gurus and to spirituality in general. In the west the common people sneer at all things mystical but, in India, people on the spiritual path are respected and listened to.

There were many good spiritual people in India but, just like in all cultures, there are also many wicked people who will exploit the vulnerable and hoodwink the credulous. In East and West there are also many spiritual conmen and charlatans and, as I have warned already, most Naadi reads, in general, are corrupt. I was hoping that, on my return to the UK, I could somehow bring back the best of India and, in my own life, combine it with the best of western mysticism, science and philosophy. I was full of hope to make the best of both worlds.

Before leaving for India I had spoken to a friend who was very excited by some séances she had attended, in which physical mediumship was manifesting. My friend was an intelligent, spiritual and very sincere individual who would never try to trick anyone or mislead people. She stuck me as someone who was not easily duped. The mediums séances were booked solid for years ahead but she pulled a few strings for me and I was able to book places for Jane and myself at a number of physical mediumship events. The first was local to me and was planned just a few weeks after my return from

India. This would be tremendously interesting for, if it was real, I could get some direct insight from the spirit world and maybe have the chance to ask about some of the incredible spiritual things that had recently happened to me.

I've worked as a medium for most of my life but have always been a little suspicious of physical mediums. Physical mediumship takes place in a dark séance room and gives direct and tangible objective proof of life after death. The physical forms that it takes can include transfiguration, direct voice, apports and levitation, rapping noises, spirit lights and the production of ectoplasm from the medium's mouth and ears. The problem with all of these miraculous phenomena is that they can easily be faked.

In Gordon Higginson's case, he would materialize full human figures made of a luminous ectoplasm that would walk around the dark séance room. Their faces were easily recognized by the sitters and the materialized spirits would talk about events from their time on earth and provide the sitters with a great deal of comforting proofs of survival of death.

Early in my career I had the good fortune to meet Gordon Higginson, a number of times, when he was the president of the National Union of Spiritualists. His demonstrations at the churches were always highly polished and incredibly accurate. Gordon was a man who could fill the room with the aura of presence. He was charming, educated and spoke many times to Jane and me about our mediumship, and encouraged us both tremendously.

A good friend of mine – who was hard to fool, was a member of MENSA and very outspoken if she saw psychic imposters – watched the figure of her mother materialize at one of Gordon Higginson's physical séances. She explained to me that she saw her mother's shining face appear in front of her and that it was instantly recognizable and not the stuff of imagination or trickery. "Only I knew what my mother looked like," she said to me "and I know my mother when I see her".

In the library area of Spiritualism's headquarters at Stansted Hall, just north of London, Gordon Higginson would regularly demonstrate this incredible physical mediumship. In a test séance, on 15th November 1974 at Stansted Hall, his generation of ectoplasm was captured by infrared photography. I never had the chance to join one of his séances but I was able to watch him demonstrate mental mediumship many times. I've watched him give mediumistic demonstrations, from the rostrum, that were simply mind-blowing. He could give the Christian and Surname of the spirit communicator every time, give highly detailed messages that included the address where the dead person lived, telephone numbers, quirks about the spirit's life and character and would sometimes boggle our brains by telling us the exact amount of money that was in our wallet or purse. Gordon Higginson gave 100% proof of life after death through his mental mediumship so I am inclined to believe that his physical mediumship was just as reliable.

Sadly, when he died in 1993, I and many other Spiritualist mediums thought that this man, who was so full of great warmth, humor and charisma, was perhaps the last of the great physical mediums and we'd never see this phenomenon again.

When Gordon Higginson became ill and eventually died, other mediums wanted to fill the vacuum and there was a scramble from some less credible physical mediums to fill his shoes. The most shocking allegations came in 1992 when the medium Colin Fry was exposed in the spiritualist newspaper *Psychic News* when he was caught allegedly faking physical mediumship, and there was a major investigation within spiritualism. Fry, who at one time performed under the stage name of "Lincoln", was caught out at a pitch black séance when the lights were unexpectedly turned on and he was seen holding a spirit trumpet in the air, which the audience had been led to believe was being levitated by spiritual energy.

The new physical mediums, emerging at the time of writing this, hail from the Noah's Ark Society, which had been formed under the instruction of a spirit communication from a discarnate spirit called Noah Zerdin, who had been a well-known spiritualist in life and the mentor of another great physical medium called Leslie Flint. Colin Fry had been active within the Noah's Ark society so Jane and I were a little suspicious of any mediums associated with it.

Colin Fry had claimed that his exposure was the result of an 'intruding entity' that had taken him over during the séance and claimed that the ties (tiewraps) holding him could have been broken by himself and could be shown to have snapped rather than cut. Dr Jim White at Newcastle-upon-Tyne University examined the ties and agreed that one bond has been sawn, but was unable to reach a conclusion about the second break. In my opinion, paranormally broken ties and an intruding entity taking over the medium is not a very convincing argument. If 'intruding entities' really were involved it is worrying as the mediumship channel is impure and may be potentially dangerous and subject to other demonic influences.

Colin Fry was exposed by spiritualists in *Psychic News* and, for a time, was banned from working publically but, as the evidence surrounding the broken ties was inconclusive, he was given the benefit of the doubt, resumed his work within spiritualism, and went on to have his own TV show and another with the medium Derek Acorah. Although I was highly suspicious of Colin Fry's physical mediumship, this was done at an early stage in his career and may have been his being foolish and a little too eager to make a name for himself.

In my opinion, Colin Fry was an average clairaudient medium who was, perhaps, tempted by the fast track to glory that the miracles of physical mediumship give. He had the gift of mediumship and some of his stage demonstrations show that he was able to give evidential proof of survival. He died from lung cancer at the age of 53 yet, despite relentless attacks from skeptics for him to confess his trickery, he faced death bravely and with an unrelenting faith in the afterlife. The Daily Telegraph obituary recounts how, as a heavy smoker, he recalled an earlier encounter with a fellow spiritualist, who disapproved: "This old love said to me: 'That'll kill you, you know.' I replied: 'My love, do you honestly think that bothers me? I know where I'm going.'"

Jane and I were clearly full of doubts about whether modern physical mediumship was something we wanted to investigate. In the early days of spiritualism there were clearly some physical mediums who were fakes and others whom had been falsely accused. A few days before we were to go to the séances, I was looking at some of the photographs from the séances of the medium Helen Duncan and thinking about how unconvincing they looked. Helen McCrae Duncan (25 November 1897 – 6 December 1956) was a Scottish medium best known as the last person to be imprisoned under the British Witchcraft Act of 1735. She was famous for producing ectoplasm which, the skeptics claimed, was regurgitated cheesecloth. From some of the pictures this certainly seems to be the case. The writer Colin Wilson and others have argued that it may be the case that Helen Duncan could produce ectoplasm but the pressures to perform had tempted her occasionally to fake her phenomena. She was not a particularly intelligent person – and some reports say she could be coarse and vulgar – so perhaps she didn't understand that to fake phenomena just the once would discredit every other real materialization she'd ever done.

Soon after looking at the images and thinking what a con physical mediumship may have been, one of Jane's sitters, who had come to our house for a reading, spontaneously started chatting about Helen Duncan. This man had been coming to see us regularly for years and lived in Portsmouth, where Helen Duncan had done many of her séances. We know him to be a very successful businessman, who intelligent, kind and sincere.

Without realizing that we were thinking about Helen Duncan and our upcoming physical séance, his conversation led to his childhood memories of his relative (I think he said Uncle), who was a policeman in Portsmouth at the time of Helen Duncan. The policeman held a high office and, for a time, had been part of the close security for Princess Elizabeth and Princess Margaret when they visited Portsmouth. Our spiritualist friend had even been invited along, as a toddler, to the Mayor's house and was allowed to play with the two princesses.

When Jane's client was a boy, the family often spoke about his uncle's most interesting case, which was to be part of the team that were to arrest the medium, Helen Duncan. During World War II, in November 1941, Helen Duncan held a séance, in Portsmouth, at which she claimed the spirit materialization of a sailor told her that HMS Barham had been sunk. Because the sinking of HMS Barham was revealed, in strict confidence, only to the relatives of casualties, and not announced to the public until late January 1942, the Navy started to take an interest in her activities and eventually decided that she was a danger to morale and should be made to shut up. Our sitter's policeman relative was part of the undercover team that would interrupt the séance and arrest Helen Duncan.

From here things get messy for the police: reports claim that, when the undercover police burst into the séance on 19 January 1944, to arrest her, a white-shrouded manifestation appeared that proved to be Duncan herself, in a white cloth, which she attempted to conceal when discovered. But this was not quite what the policeman had witnessed himself for, as he barged into the darkened séance room, he reached out to grab the 'cheesecloth' that was pouring out of the medium's mouth and, as he grabbed it, the material evaporated and disappeared through his fingers. This event deeply affected and puzzled him for the rest of his life. Perhaps his conscience was troubled, too, for what was reported in court differs profoundly from what really happened.

As you will gather, Jane and I had mixed feelings about what lay ahead at the first physical mediumship that I'd booked. At best, Jane hoped for a clear message from her friend who had recently died and I was looking hoping to get some interesting insights into my mystic journey to India. (I will not be naming these mediums in this edition of the book – let's call this one 'Medium X'.)

The séance took place, a few miles from our home, in the garden of a private house where they'd built a large soundproofed shed especially for the séances. Before we went in we were made to sign a disclaimer form, show picture ID and asked to remove any metal objects. It was quite an expensive event of about 20 guest sitters paying £40 per head. We were told that the medium would take no money except travel expenses – which was encouraging – and the balance of the evening's takings would be used to support the venue that, we noticed, was undergoing extensive alterations. But, hey, £80 for Jane and me to witness the priceless miracles of physical mediumship is well worth it!

The medium sat in one corner of the room and beneath his chair were various crystals, stones and bowls of water that, we were told, would help to build his energy. He asked Jane to sit next to him and I was sitting across the room. We were warned that there will be loud music to build the energy and that the red light will be switched off after the first two tracks. The main lights were turned off and we were blasted with ear-splitting music from Queen: "I want to break free!!!" It was deafening.

In Edwardian physical circles, they used to sing hymns to build the energy but being blasted, in what by now was pitch black, seemed complete madness. Then we had a load of Indian music – Hiawatha music as Jane called it – and the medium dropped into trance. His spirit guide came through when the music stopped and we were greeted by a working class Victorian man, from the North of England, talking through him and telling us about his life: "I was a baddun I was. Eeeee. I weren't very nice. I used to hit my wife. I used to spend all my pennies in the pub I did," and so on. No verifiable spirit evidence.

But the real treat was yet to come as loads of famous people came clambering through, all keen to talk to us nobodies and share their banal discourses. We were treated to poor impersonations of William Crookes the spiritualist scientist – who, I would have hoped, could have revealed some scientific information – a ridiculous speech from Sir Winston Churchill who, sadly, was now speaking with a northern accent and had completely lost his eloquence and, of course, we heard from Michael Jackson and many others who came to share their mad discourses. Clearly the spirit world is a sort of asylum.

For the Grand Finale we were blasted with the music of Louis Armstrong and, when it stopped, had Louis talk to us in his croaky voice with a Yorkshire accent! He didn't sing, thank God, but he did ask one of the women to get up and dance with him in the pitch black. And this is the real miracle: she did get up and waltzed around the ink dark room to the bellowing music while hugged tight by the invisible ghost of Louis Armstrong. If I'd put my leg out, she'd be dead!

"Can you feel me holding you?" spoke Louis through the medium.

"Oh yes Louis I can, can!" she replied.

We were then able to experience some other phenomena such as a psychic breeze, but not convincing as I could hear the medium blowing hard from his side of the room. This was followed by some clairgustance in which the blowing noises were not disguised this time but we could clearly smell something on his breath, which I assume, was a sweet or capsule he'd bitten into. By this time my bowels were feeling a little active and I was very, very tempted to return the favor with a little special clairgustance of my own.

Jane was sitting next to him and, with his free foot that wasn't tied to the chair, he stepped on her foot and said "Can anyone feel spirit touching them?" She remained quiet as he pushed harder on her foot and repeated the question. Jane knew what he was up to and kept quiet for there is nothing a fraud likes more than a testimonial from someone genuine.

I have not mentioned the medium's name, as he was a very nice man who genuinely believed in what he was saying but, in my opinion, is not a real medium. As far as I could tell, none of the sitters were deeply bereaved so no real harm was done and this nonsense will clearly not convince anyone sensible about the reality of the spirit world. Some people are easily satisfied by these entertaining antics but they are totally lacking in any genuine evidence of spirit communication. In my opinion this is delusional behavior with a little mass hysteria thrown in. I see, from his website, that he is booked all over the world so you could be in for a treat, too.

If this were a restaurant I would have demanded my money back but I asked Jane to say nothing as I had other séances booked with other physical mediums and I didn't want to get banned. We smiled, said 'thank you for a lovely evening', and drove home with ringing ears. "First time you've taken me out for ages and you've exposed me to Louis Armstrong, Freddy Mercury, Lord Dowding, Oscar Wilde... everyone except Mary bloody Poppins," spluttered Jane. "I feel I've been taken on some weird drug trip. Don't take me anywhere like that again!"

The next physical mediumship séance I had planned for us to visit was in Kent and this was going to be a long drive from our home. This medium came with a number of good testimonials, including one from a friend of ours who is a solicitor – an astute man who, in his retirement, has been investigating physical mediumship and has received compelling evidence for the continuation of life after death from a number of physical mediums.

The organizers of the event appeared to be sincere people but, again, it was quite expensive at £50 per head with about 60 people or more in attendance. Before going into the small hall, where the séance itself would take place, we were briefed about what would happen and how we must remove all metal objects and would be searched before we entered the room where the séance would take place. Everyone was expected to project their psychic energy and this would be particularly enhanced tonight, as five of the regular sitters from the medium's home circle would be there to add to the spiritual energy.

When we went into the small hall where the séance itself was to take place, we were all carefully searched and a metal detector run over us to ensure that no metal items were missed. I was then invited to run the metal detector over the medium and anyone else who, I felt, might be concealing anything metallic. Rings that could not be removed were wrapped in bandages to prevent them from harming the medium's energy. It seemed a little odd to me that so much fuss was made about removing all metal. During the introductory talk we had been told that any metal in the room – including night vision cameras – could disrupt the ectoplasm and may cause burns to the medium and yet I noted that the medium was sitting just in front of a large air-conditioning unit and there were plenty of other metallic items in the room such as pipes, door handles and radiators. As I understood it, it was the medium who must be divested of metal, not the sitters.

The medium directed us, one by one, to our seats to ensure a 'balanced distribution of the energy in the circle'. He sat Jane and me apart, with me sitting close to him at the top end of the circle. The medium was tied securely to the chair with plastic ties threaded through a woolen pullover that was looped with ties from behind like a straightjacket. Houdini would have loved it.

I was then asked to examine everything closely and to mark the ties with a marker pen so that I could verify that they are the same ties afterwards. I also examined the chair to make sure there were no trick catches, and so on. I was asked to check the size of the medium's hands. Finally, I was asked to announce to the people present that I was reassured that the medium was securely tied and that, in my opinion, there was no way he could escape. I'm not sure if I was selected at random or whether they had chosen me do this because they knew that I am a well-known medium, write regularly for *Psychic News* and my word would add credibility to the proceedings. I know a lot about the spiritual mechanics of mediumship but nothing about the mechanics of escapology so, in this instance, my word was as good as anyone's.

When the medium was fully secured we were all told to tuck our feet in under the chair, hold hands and were then plunged into a pitch-black abyss of darkness. As I sat holding hands in the dark with a large red-faced 'artistic' looking man, we were now blasted with music and asked to sing along to Judy Garland's 'Over the Rainbow' followed by Freddy Mercury and other awful songs. When the music stopped there was loud clap of the hands and the medium talked to us in a guttural, posh voice with a Victorian accent – the same voice I note that Colin Fry and others would use in their physical and trace work. We were treated to an address of simplistic spiritualist philosophy about the way things are in the spirit world and a discourse about how foolish we are to keep demanding proof of the spirit communicators. This particularly discourse rubbed me up the wrong way for, without evidence and verifiable proofs, spiritualism is worthless.

We all had to supply photos and fill out forms and disclaimers before joining the circle so the medium could get access to this information and this could have compromised any evidence given in the session. The woman, whose hand I was holding on my left, was clearly very distressed and was desperately hoping for a message from her son. She was part of an Indian family group of six who, I learned later, had travelled all this way by taxi from London. All of them would have filled in forms so it is likely that one of them would have made a comment. The medium's voice now offered a message from her son in the voice of what sounded like a mildly distressed eight-year-old boy. He told mummy that he was out of pain and everything was all right with him. A few other things were said but, from what I heard, there was nothing included that could be taken as proof of the spirit communicator. When he finished I quietly asked in the lady how old her son was when he died: "Twenty Two", she whispered in reply. The father of the son who was sitting on the opposite side to us commented that they had come all that way and their son had only so few words to say.

Fortunately the Victorian man speaking through the medium had lots more to say but, in my opinion, none of it was proof of spirit or particularly inspiring. And, of course, some famous people came through including, yes you've got it, Louis Armstrong who apparently was very upset that other mediums were impersonating him. (Clearly the first medium we'd seen had seen this show, too.)

A few more spirit messages followed for members of the circle but it was apparent that these were regular guests who took it for granted that it was their relatives communicating from spirit. There was no evidence of survival, just messages that the sitters lapped up. It struck me that these people were not in cahoots with the medium but were simply gullible people who readily accepted messages without first demanding some form of proof of identity from the spirit communicator.

When the 'clairvoyance' was over, we were thrown, again, into more loud music and an invisible spirit would walk around the room. When the music stopped we could hear his footsteps in the blackness, which then stopped in front of me. The Victorian spirit man said that he was going to touch my head with his hand, which he placed on my cranium and then spread his hand to its full width. "You will note that my hand is bigger than the medium's hand that you examined earlier," he said.

A hand spread over your head will seem bigger but all of this could be a simple distraction as there was no proof that this was a spirit, the hand felt normal, and no proof that this was the medium who may have untied himself. All this was followed by a number of floating objects and a luminous trumpet that floated around the room and spun in a circle – if it was on a string this would be easy to accomplish. Finally we were told that the medium's chair was now going to float above us on ectoplasm rods. All went silent, followed by a loud crash in the middle of the circle. A few moments later the lights were turned on to reveal the medium securely tied to his chair in the middle of the room.

Everyone was amazed, of course, and nobody could fathom how the medium had allegedly levitated and crashed into the centre of the circle. I was asked to examine the marks on the ties and it was clear to me that these were the same as I had made earlier. Also it was pointed out that the medium's tied pullover was now on back to front.

It took Jane and me some time to work out if trickery had happened but it became clear as we drove home and discussed our experiences. This was a simple case of what the magicians call misdirection. A great deal of fuss had been made to make sure that the ties were all secure and that the medium could not escape but all that happened that evening could have been done by one of the medium's confederates. There were three or four people from his home circle who helped with the searches and who could have used me to distract people should they want to bring things into the room such as night vision goggles. (These would not necessarily be needed if the confederates practiced in advance and counted their footsteps in the dark.)

Everyone held hands to 'build the energy' but this, of course, served to stop anyone touching the spirits walking around the room and also gave the illusion that everyone was seated. If five confederates sat together – as they did that evening – then the two on the outside could continue to hold the visiting guests hands while the three in the middle were free to let go and move around the room at will. In the booming music they would not be heard as they – early on in the proceedings – moved the chair of the medium into the centre of the room ready for the grand finale. Everyone is distracted by the illusion that the voices and floating objects come from the gagged medium who couldn't possibly do all these things. But, of course, his cohorts could do all the voices and other chicanery on his behalf. At the end, when the heavy chair is allegedly high in the air, all the others need do is angle the chair backwards and let it crash forward giving the illusion that it's fallen from a great height.

As Jane and I drove home, we were both fuming at the deceptions that we saw and have now made our views known to prominent spiritualists (though it has to be said that these people act outside of spiritualism that now insists that night vision cameras are always to be used at physical séances). What most upset us was the utter contempt and cruelty that this group of people showed towards the Indian party who were clearly very bereaved and confused by what they had seen.

Terrible grief and disappointment was evident on their faces and in their eyes.

I have complained how sometimes the Indian Naadi oracles are being misused; now here was an example of how western mediumship is being misused in the worst possible way. The spiritual seeker sometimes treads a perilous path with scoundrels lurking at every turn of the road.

CHAPTER 16

ॐ

Bhrigu Rishi Records

After my return from India I suffered from signs of septicemia that the doctor spotted quickly and cleared up with a course of antibiotics. As part of my research for this book, and to get insight into my health with the help of contacts Kim knew in India, I consulted an astrological oracle called the Bhrigu Samhita. On a deeper level I was looking for more confirmation of ways to be of service to the spirit and to be sure of the next steps to take in sharing with others the knowledge of the Naadis and Samhitas.

The Bhrigu Samhita is an astrological treatise attributed to Maharishi Bhrigu that is claimed to have been written 10,000 years ago in the Treta Yuga and, just like the Naadi oracles, the Bhrigu Samhita contains predictions about a person's current and future lives as well as information on their past life.

The Bhrigu Samhita is very similar in many ways to the Naadi leaves in that it contains very personal information, which the sage Bhrigu dictated from his clairvoyant insight into what western Theosophists call the Akashic Records, that is said to contain the records of every human being who ever lived or will live on earth. And, just like the Naadi Oracle, the Bhrigu Samhita has many imitators. As Kali Yuga continues, the forces of darkness eclipse the forces of light and the once great art of Indian Astrology is today dominated by charlatans and cheats. Today there are just a few left, who devote themselves to the discipline and dedication demanded to master the ancient knowledge, and fewer still have undergone the penances and challenges required to master the Bhrigu Naadi.

I was lucky, again, as Kim had done the legwork back in June 1993 when he found the oracle on his way to a man called Vijay Bhushan Sharma, who lives on the outskirts of New Delhi and has a good Bhrigu Samhita collection that consists of several hundred thousand horoscopes and is said to weigh several tons. It is kept in a building separate from his main residence and, at one time, a large fire devastated all the surrounding houses but left the collection completely unscathed. The collection had been passed down through the family for generations.

The current astrologer that Kim uses is a woman and all I needed to send her was my birth data. Kim informed me that the readings with the Bhrigu Samhita are usually quite short but accurate and give information about just the most important things in as direct a way as possible. The seeker is usually given some remedies that they can perform themselves. From Naadi experiences Kim describes, some of the texts, such as the Ganesh Naadi, can be very elaborate and entwined with grand mythology that seems exaggerated and is hard for the western mind to grasp. I looked forward to receiving my simple but precise reading from the Bhrigu Samhita.

The sage Shri Bhrigu is one of the ancient seven sages (Sapta Rishi) of India who were mentioned in the Mahabharata and entrusted with the task of maintaining righteousness on earth. Bhrigu is credited as the father of Hindu astrology and is the primary author of the Bhrigu Samhita. Legends say that he was the wish-born-son (Manasaputra) of Lord Brahma who simply wished him into existence.

One of the meanings of the Sanskrit word *Samhita* is a 'rule-based combination of text or verses' so it is likely that the Bhrigu Samhita was compiled over a long period of time by a number of contributors. The original treatise is said to have contained over 5 million horoscopes but only about 50,000 survive. As with the Naadi libraries, many of the Bhrigu Samhita collections were destroyed by foreign invasions and, in particular, by the sacking of ancient Nalanda University that was destroyed by the Muslim army led by the Turkish leader Bakhtiyar Khilji in 1193. Many of the Bhrigu Samhita manuscripts were taken away to foreign countries.

Fortunately my horoscope had survived. The full transcript is in the appendix but I will now comment on the accuracy of my reading. The text starts by describing my past life, which is different from the past lives described in the Naadi oracles. As we all have a number of past lives, I presume this is one life of many. In this past life I was born in a low caste but had contact with local kings and, because of these contacts, made a lot of money. With wealth, my own behavior deteriorated and I became egotistical and corrupt and said many bad things about the king, the officials and the priests.

This was all very different from the saintly lives that my Naadis had spoken about but also rang true. Before discovering the Naadis I'd had a number of intuitive feelings about my past lives and this information seemed immediately to correspond with a dream I'd had some years ago. The dream was simple but so vivid and unexpected that it had stayed with me. I was sitting in a Roman bathhouse joking about the Emperor, whom I was calling Vespasian, and his Flavian Fools. We were howling with laughter about what a fool he was and how we had all benefited from this idiot and though his stupidity had gained lands and wealth.

I had had other dreams about Ancient Rome before, but this one was so incredibly real and vivid that I awoke shaking. Could it be that the king I had cheated in my past life was the Emperor in my dream? I read that Vespasian was far from being a fool, and was a commanding personality and very witty, but there were also many conspiracies against him during his reign and detractors were punished in his newly built showpiece, the Colosseum. If this was a past life I was certainly taking a lot of risks!

Because of these insincere activities in my past life, the oracle says I "will have doubts and dubious ideas of what is real spirituality and what is not, so in accordance with his fate he will face troubles in regards also to his destiny's growth." This is true to the extent that, throughout my life, I have been very angered by fake mediums, idiotic ghost hunters and pompous psychics with silly ideas who distract from the real truths that underpin Spiritualism and spirituality. I also seem to have to fight twice as hard to achieve my goals. As an antidote to my transgressions I am to say 'Om Namo Bhagvate Vasudevaya' daily. This is the mantra of Vishnu and Krishna both. It can be chanted like Gayatri Mantra and is the principal mantra of the Vedic scripture 'Srimad Bhagavatam'. I consider it a lovely mantra to chant.

What it had to say about me as a person was interesting and mostly correct but it was not a baffling mind-warp like the Naadi leaves. It said I am 'quite brilliant' which, I guess, is right as I am talented in many fields but that could be the sort of flattery you'd find in cold readings. It said I would not enjoy peaceful sleep, which was right at the time of the consultation but not generally through my life – though it has to be said that my wife Jane snores! (Don't tell her I told you.) It went on to say that I have big dreams but am not successful with my ambitions, which is not quite true as I have achieved more in life than the average person, although I have had many opportunities snatched from me by others, particularly with my work on TV. One medium – now dead – even stole the script and treatment that I'd written for our own psychic show, presented it to a channel as his idea and used the exact words from my sample script as the opening presentation for his first show.

Two things did jump out from the short text. One was where it said "This person is blessed with a sixth sense and many miracles like things will come to happen in this life and God always support him." This is true. The other was the line: "This person will also have lot of properties and land in this present life." This is not the case but it is interesting that it is the same as the prophecies given to be by the Naadi and also by the Siddha yogi. I am not ambitious about having this but maybe it is a reaffirmation that I should push our ideas for a foundation and spiritual centres forward. At the time of writing, we have a foundation set up and enough donations to become a registered charity but certainly not enough to buy land or property.

The Bhrigu Samhita next gives a date by date account of my life, which to some extent was true, but in places I felt I had to make the facts fit. Clearly this is not the 100% accuracy that I was seeing in the Naadis but maybe I'd been spoilt.

It gave a long list of illnesses that I should be suffering from now but, as I do yoga, I am very healthy apart from a few minor and manageable problems. The text also mentioned "Pre-deaths risk/dangers are there, accidents, police custody, and defamation, loss of respect or prestige are there in life" but this, as Kim pointed out, could be a warning for the future. The Naadi mentioned that I may be falsely accused of something by a 'conspiracy of women'.

Although it was right about the times of my marriages, education and the birth of one of my children, it appeared to be wrong about a lot of what it said such as: a risk of an operation at age two, an accident at age 3, father leaving between ages of 5 and 7 (Father was loyal to my mum all his life), mother having a serious illness at my age 9, health problems between ages 19 and 21, career starting at age 22 (I lived in a Kibbitz at that age), up to age 25 threats from fire (never happened), between ages 31 and 40 will get a child (I was 27 when my first daughter was born, though a second child was born when I was 35) and between ages of 40 and 41 health problems will start (I have had no serious health problems throughout my life).

The Bhrigu was right on quite a few things but had not been as accurate as the Naadi oracles I'd consulted before. At this time I also discovered that some of the Naadi readers I had used in the past were now charging extraordinary amounts for their readings and remedies so it was clear that these were now corrupted and could not be used anymore. Once money and greed infects the readers then the Naadi predictions falter and may no longer prove accurate.

Fortunately the Bhrigu appeared to remain pure and was only charging small fees for their services so I decided to have another try and, this time, consult the Bhrigu Prashna Naadi and, from the same source, I would access my Maha Muni Agasthyar Jeeva Naadi. The Bhrigu Prashna Naadi requires 5 questions from me about aspects of my life. Initially I asked if I could ask 5 questions about the future of the world but apparently this is no longer permitted as too may predictions have been ignored.

During my researches I was told of a number of revelations made by the Bhrugu Samhita, which gave important prophecies that were not heeded. Rajiv Gandhi, who was the Prime Minister of India, serving from 1984 to 1989, was warned by the oracle not to visit a specific market place as otherwise he would get killed. His office said the security was optimal and so forth. Rajiv Gandhi's last public meeting was on 21 May 1991, at Sriperumbudur, a village approximately 40 km (25 mi) from Madras, where he was assassinated while campaigning for the Sriperumbudur Lok Sabha Congress candidate. At 10:10 pm, a woman, later identified as Thenmozhi Rajaratnam, approached Gandhi in public and greeted him. She then bent down to touch his feet and detonated a belt laden with 700 g (1.5 lb) of RDX explosives tucked under her dress. The explosion killed Gandhi, Rajaratnam, and at least 25 other people.

Similarly, there was a case in which 'another President of India' (I presume this was Fakhruddin Ali Ahmed) was warned by Bhrigu about a severe health problem, and that he needed to do certain things, but the advice was ignored and he died of illness while still in office. There are similar ignored warnings described by the Sri Agastyar Jeeva Naadi readers.

The most interesting Naadi revelation that people in the UK will find interesting is the case of the missing, then three-year-old child, Madelaine McCann. She disappeared on the evening of 3 May 2007 from her bed in a holiday apartment in Praia da Luz, a resort in the Algarve region of Portugal, sparking what one newspaper called "the most heavily reported missing-person case in modern history". Very specific descriptions were given in the leaves about what happened and why it happened. The parents, police and others were informed properly but all in vain. As far as I am aware the leaves are still there but the details will only be released again either to the police or, better still, to the parents.

The readers tell us that it is a waste of time pursuing information that will not be heard or is not ready yet to be revealed to the world. What the Rishis say in the leaves is that they are there for all those people who are truly seeking to know their destiny but they will not simply contact people with the information. People must earnestly seek out the Rishis though the leaves. It strikes me as a case of: 'Seek and you will find – but we're not just dropping it on your lap!'

The first oracle to be given me was the 5 questions I'd asked the Bhrigu Prashna Naadi. I'd decided to ask 5 questions about the progress of the media work, my work as a psychic medium, deepening my spiritual practice, progressing my charity work and how to cure my tinnitus. To my surprise the oracle simply gave me a list of remedies, some of which could be performed by a Brahmin priest and the rest by me. There were some strange things included such as feeding the birds every day to speed up the sale of the TV series and to cure my tinnitus I was to make a special paste from peppers and a few other strange ingredients and put it on my forehead. I was also told to walk daily to the river for a month and throw a small packet of flour into it while chanting a mantra.

I made a start by feeding the birds and, to my amazement, a call came through on the same day with our first sale to a small channel in the Czech Republic in Central Europe. It was a small start but now our distributor could tell buyers in Cannes that the program has sales.

A week later a typed transcript of the Maha Muni Agasthyar Jeeva Naadi was sent to me by email from Northern India. This contained some very interesting and specific insights into my life but did not have the 'wow factor' of other Naadis that I'd consulted, which included my name, ex-wife's name, wife's name, mother's name, father's name and so on. For this reason I was concerned that the Naadi may simply be an astrology reading, which was based upon my birthdate and corresponded with the things already given to me in earlier Naadi readings. It said 'He will achieve what he has set himself up to do through some foreign partner,' which is right in that a sale was already being negotiated in the Czech Republic via our Canadian Distributor based in California. It also said elsewhere in the text 'He will gain much luck and support through a foreigner who is also having the Yoga Bhagya'. Soon after getting the reading I was approached unexpectedly by a German Publisher who offered to publish my books in Germany. Yoga Bhagya means 'yoga luck' – my publisher had also independently been given a message through the Naadi leaves some years ago and practised the yoga taught by Paramahansa Yogananda.

The answers to my five questions for the Bhriugu Prashna Naadi did feel to me as if they were remedies drawn from a hat. The Bhruguji Prashna Naadi had some good information but not the mind-boggling facts, which I'd come to expect from my previous consultations. I don't feel there was any cheating going on. It could have been possible to frame a Naadi reading around the five questions I'd asked earlier but not to have 'seen' the overseas contacts it mentioned. And, finally, the cost for to do the remedies was sky high as each one required four Brahmins, a lot of time and the hire of a temple. In view of all this it was decided to have just the most important remedies done by four independent Brahmins at the Trimbakeshwar Shiva Temple in the town of Trimbak, in the Nashik District of Maharashtra, India.

There was nothing untoward going on with this oracle but it does, again, make me want to remind the reader of the pitfalls that can sometimes accompany Naadi readings. We used independent people to do the remedies so as to take away the potential for big profits from the Naadi reader. The amounts asked for remedies can sometimes run into thousands of dollars so, from a corrupt Naadi reader's point of view, he would only need to hook a few people to secure a very good living. The scams I witnessed with the physical mediumship, that I wrote about in an earlier chapter, are a sobering reminder of the lengths to which people will go to extract money form spiritual seekers. I was in the fortunate position of being able independently to commission reliable Brahmins but, of course, if you are treading these waters alone you may be at the mercy of the Naadi reader.

CHAPTER 17

ॐ

Naadi Shocks

We are all divine spirits who live temporarily within a human body. The spirit is, in turn, linked to the whole universe in an endless mycelium of astral energy that resonates in every tiny unit of existence as well as in the infinite cosmos. What we are, is a miniature expression of the totality of the Universe and, although the planets and stars in themselves do not determine a person's destiny, we are nonetheless intimately connected to their vibrations.

According to Indian astrology, the exact time of our birth is determined by our past karma and we are reborn at a time that is in perfect harmony with the positions of the planets and stars from the moment of our conception. The proper use of astrology is to reveal our karma and from this find the best ways to take on the challenges of our destiny. In India they also use a different system from western astrology that is based on the sidereal or visible zodiac. This system allows for the shift of the equinoxes by a correction called ayanamsa. (The difference between the Vedic and the Western zodiacs is currently around 24 degrees.) Indian astrology is usually much more fatalistic than western astrology. It does not always allow for the possibility of free will to fix things.

The stars do not determine our fate but are just a reflection of our destiny that is made by our past karma. This individual karma is affected for good or bad by the vibrations of the heavenly bodies that interact with our astral body through the chakras (spiritual centres) in the spinal column. The chakras in the astral body are connected by channels called nadi – which is a word from the Sanskrit root nad meaning "channel", "stream", or "flow". Nadis are the channels through which the life force flows through the astral body and particularly within the spinal column. The flow of these spiritual energies are influences by the planets and stars and are identified in Nadi Astrology, the Bhrigu Samhita and the Naadi palm leaf oracles.

Karma governs the stars, and with it our destiny, but also karma can be influenced by our free will and determination to become divinely conscious beings. So, when it seems that our horoscope deals us a bad hand, we would be wise to see this as a revelation of our karma and then to take actions to eradicate negative karmic effects. We should also take on the task of self-transformation with enthusiasm, knowing that our destiny can also be changed by our spiritual efforts. Negative radiations and adverse astrological influences will have less effect on a person who is doing spiritual work or is building their spiritual resources through yoga, pranayama and meditation. It is one more reason not to destroy one's life with impure living, wrong thinking, poor diet, drinking excessive alcohol and bad company.

The treasure of the true Naadi readings is that not only is the past karma revealed but also a remedy is given by the sages to counter any negative karma. Astrology alone can sometimes paralyze a person's free choice if it is not also accompanied by some method of eradicating the bad karma. The stars cannot help us but if we determinedly follow a spiritual path and seek divine revelation in our own lives then even the stars shall touch our feet, for there is nothing greater than the power of God working through us.

The Naadi palm leaves are a form of astrology that has been given to us by Self-realized rishis and not from the superficial astrologers of the market place. Even when a negative destiny and dark karma is revealed, the sages find a remedy to help us to mitigate the disastrous effects of sins done in past lives. This was the case of Wendy who, we were to discover though her Naadis, had poisoned her brother in a past life and now was about to pay the price.

Wendy's strange reading

Wendy had worked for a major pharmaceutical company as their marketing manager and wanted to sell their cosmetics ranges into the rapidly growing 'mystical market'. The unique selling point of the cosmetic range they were launching was that it had many bright and cheerful colours and she approached me with the idea of doing a press release around the idea of choosing the right cosmetic colours to match your aura. For the launch I gave aura readings to the visiting journalists and they went away and – hopefully – wrote a glowing report about the new cosmetic colours on offer.

The campaign was a huge success in a highly competitive area where every manufacturer was fighting to get positive exposure in the fashion news columns and magazines. The readings were so popular that the company decided to include my spot every year to encourage the journalists to attend. I was a sort of spiritual bait.

During these events Wendy and some of the other bosses had readings from me and, of course, a simple aura reading, more often than not, turned into a full-on mediumistic session. Wendy says she had a great deal of help from this and other readings she later had with me:

> I first met Craig when we hired him to do aura readings at a press event we were holding for a big retailer. Craig came in to our office and literally amazed us. We asked him for a demonstration – he looked at a colleague and saw red around her tummy and said you're pregnant – this lady was only 6 weeks and hadn't told a soul. He then looked at another colleague and saw red around her mouth, said she had toothache which again was true.
>
> On the day of the event Craig had a queue from the back of the room waiting to see him. Every single journalist who came out was in shock at his accuracy and most of his aura readings turned into spiritual readings as Craig had connected with someone, who had passed, connected to the person having the reading.
>
> I eventually asked if I could have a reading and I can honestly say if I was skeptical before I certainly wasn't after the reading. Without my saying a word, apart from occasionally saying 'yes' or 'no', he came up with some amazing things.
>
> He explained he couldn't do an aura reading as my Nan was in the room. He described her and, yes, she could have been any old woman but, as he went on, it became scarily true. My mum was having a troubled marriage and was considering divorce, without my saying anything. Craig said "your nan says your mum is considering divorce and is highly stressed; please tell her I'm with her and everything will be ok."
>
> He went on to tell me that I had to ask my mum about a family secret that no one knew about. He said it involved an Italian

prisoner of war and my Nan. When I did ask my mum after the reading she burst into tears as this was true: my Nan had an affair and we all had brown eyes, unlike anyone else in her family.

He then ran through many more things including describing in great detail the big tree in my front garden and how it would affect my flat. That I was going to move to a house with the number 4 in it (my house is 54) and that I had a useless boyfriend who was draining my resources and I needed to get rid of him.

I recently had a reading with Craig in 2017 and again I was blown away with his accuracy. He again picked up on my dad (my dad passed 2 years ago) and how proud he was of me. But this time he picked up on my daughter whom I lost 8 years ago at the age of 5 months. He gave me comfort by clarifying that she was now with her grandad, my dad. However, he also picked up on the fact that she was taking me on a spiritual journey. This pretty much clarified what I was thinking as pre my daughter I used to worry about everything and didn't really look outside my own life and friends apart from my love of animals. Now I'm involved in helping those with cancer, charities and animals welfare. I'm drawn to people and animals and charities I want to help. This has never happened before.

During the reading Craig told me about a lady called Sam 29 who has since passed from cancer, and pretty much confirmed what I was thinking. I was drawn to helping Sam through my daughter. I wanted to be there for Sam, daily, and help her with her cancer battle. In a way it was like fighting a similar battle to the one I'd had over losing my own daughter.

Craig went on to talk about my business and other aspects of my life but, for me, the greatest comfort was the proofs I was given from those dear to me in the spirit world and the clarification I received about my spiritual feelings and why my life was changing course.

Wendy was to go on to open her own PR Company. I felt that Wendy was a person on a real spiritual quest who had a nagging feeling that there was something very important she needed to know about her life and the course it was taking. She was doing a lot of charitable work and service to others but, still, life kept dealing her hard blows. She's read my other book and asked me if maybe the Naadi oracle could help to reveal her path.

Wendy was very worried about asking the oracle a question. As I had explained to her, the Naadi does not pull its punches and will lay everything bare. She was particularly worried that it would tell her that she would have a short life and she had a persistent eerie feeling that her death was stalking her. I knew exactly how she felt: I had made my first consultation thinking that my life was soon to end.

I set up two sessions on Skype, with a reliable Naadi reader whom I knew, and Kim would keep a check on things, too, to ensure that there was no cheating or additions made to the remedies. The sessions were three-way, with Wendy, the Naadi reader and me. For the first session the leaf was found after about an hour of looking. It was towards the end of the bundle and, just as we were worrying that it would not be found, a leaf was read that had all Wendy's information on it. "Your partner's name is Nicolas, your mother's name is Shirley and your father's name is Albert. You have had three children, two living and one dead. Two children are living with you. Both are from your partner. You were born in the year 1968 on the second of January. It was a Tuesday. Sharanar is your birth star. Capricorn is your Moon Sign. Your mother is alive. Your father is dead. You have two sisters. Your first sister is married. Your second sister is in a relationship. You are getting the reading at the age of 49. This is the proof."

This was a leaf called the Maha Shiva Athisootchamam from her thumbprint identified as Mani Maguda Pinnal Reka with 5 dots.

I will not go into the details of Wendy's leaf as much of it is personal and not necessary to the thread of what I am explaining here. Suffice it to say that the leaf gave startling information, which could not have been guessed or fed back from things that had been asked earlier in the reading.

The oracle predicted the time of her death, which, fortunately, is at a ripe old age, and gave Wendy information about the course of her life. There was information about her family, relationships, health and business as well as some strange predictions about meeting Siddhi yogis, getting spirit messages from her dead parents in dreams and spending her last days on earth in a state of total silence, during which time she will be able to speak directly to God before passing away peacefully.

In the section about her past life it said that she had cheated her younger brother out of his inheritance, and poisoned him, although she repented in later life and did social service. I was interested to see how Wendy reacted to this, during the Skype session, as it all seemed to make sense to her and she felt it explained why her good efforts in this present life often flew awry. There are not many people who would like to be told that they'd committed murder in a past life but Wendy accepted it. I know that she has done a lot of sincere charitable work in this life so I'm sure she has already mitigated much of the karma. However, the Naadi did give a number of warnings and said that she was in critical danger of having a car accident that could result in surgery.

By now I was beginning to worry about the reading. It is, of course, always a possibility that the reader could sprinkle the pot with a few extra car accidents and frightening predictions to increase the remedy bill. In Europe this sort of reading breaks every rule in the Trade Descriptions Act and I certainly would not want to be a part of anything that would frighten people or extract money through fearsome prophecy. I was concerned, but pleased that I could monitor events. It was the reason I do not to give out the names of Naadi readers to people who ask but I also knew, through my own experience, that the Rishis who wrote the leaves also offer ways to change your destiny. I had used this reader myself and believed him to be legitimate.

The leaves warned that Wendy must perform her remedies, or have them performed on her behalf as soon as she can, to minimize the karmic effects carried forward from her past life. There were lots of remedies that the leaves said had to be done in India so, if they were to be done immediately, then they would need to be done by proxy. I had plans in place in advance so that Wendy, if she preferred, could use a different person to do the remedies. It was a long list that included Ayush Homam rituals, mantras, food donations and visits to temples such as Rameswaram. She trusted the reader and, once it was quoted, gave the go-ahead for him do the remedies on her behalf.

About a week into the remedies, and after some of the most important ones had been completed, I had a message from Wendy on Facebook: "Craig you are not going to believe this. I had my car crash. Tonight someone went into back of me in a minor way. If I had not had the remedy I dread to think what would have happened. I was flabbergasted. And my sister, Jackie, whom I told all about the Naadi readings, was on the phone when the man in the car behind ran into us. She was completely spooked!"

My next friend to consult the Naadi lives in India so, for her, it was not such a culture shock and she would be able to visit the temples and do the prescribed remedies herself.

Anuradha's Shocking Reading

Anuradha is a friend from a Hindu background whom I have made through FaceBook. She was born in London but lives in Calcutta. I got to know her through our mutual interest in the holy man, Sathya Sai Baba. She read my first book about the Naadi and was inspired to find her own leaves. I've never given Anu a reading but we have got to know one another though banter, chat and some spiritual discussion online.

I introduced her to some of my Naadi reader contacts but she managed to find her own reliable reader whom she could visit, face to face, in her home town of Calcutta, India.

"My friend told me about a Naadi centre in Calcutta and I was able to find the leaves relating to my family. We found the leaves within 16-19 minutes of giving the fingerprints and my young son of 19 found his within just ten minutes.

The readers knew nothing about me, and would only allow me to answer 'yes' or 'no' to the information written on the leaves, and yet they found the names and leaves for my parents, father-in-law, husband, son and myself. The reader said, without any hesitation whatsoever, the exact names of my grandparents and parents, which were very uncommon names that are not used nowadays. Even 100-140 years ago when they were born these were very obscure names. The leaves mentioned every single person's physical, mental problems, which included their emotional problems, accidents they'd had, any surgery they'd undergone as well as their exact dates of birth. The detail of one person was very different from the other, yet it was bang on target every time."

Anu had been a little worried about consulting the leaves in that she was a follower of Sathya Sai Baba and felt that seeking spiritual direction from a source other than her own guru would be a spiritual betrayal. She told her friend that she believed in and had surrendered to Baba so would not do anything without His consent. If she were to get guidance from the leaves then Baba must give her a sign and explicitly confirm His consent.

Three weeks before her visit to the Naadi reader she had a dream about Sathya Sai Baba. Devotees of Sathya Sai Baba believe that dreams of him are real meetings with the guru:

"I had a dream in which I saw myself walking down a by lane which was reminiscent of the town of Shirdi. As I was walking past a small wall, I saw Sathya Sai Baba sitting on the pavement next to other beggars, in a severely emaciated condition. I was shocked seeing Him like that and was going to run over when my son grabbed my wrist and stopped me, saying, "How can that be Baba? You see Baba everywhere and in everyone. You're always like this! That's not Baba!"

"I shook off his grip and said, "It IS Baba. Don't you come in between Him and me! You go off to where you were going, but don't stop me."

Saying this, I went over to Baba and helped Him get up and asked, "What happened to you Baba? Why are you in this state?" He stood up and said, "Look" and then whirled His hand around in the way He does when He's producing something and a small earthen statuette of the Goddess Durga appeared. As he placed her flat on His palm, I saw that the statuette was bordered all around in pure gold. He then placed His index finger on her third eye on the statue and a stream of white light started emanating from it. (It was like the white light one gets immersed in when one has a vision of God in His pure energy form – Vishwa Darshan.)

The white light started growing until the statue was invisible and all I could see was this brilliant, bright white light completely enveloping the statue.

As soon as Baba lifted His finger, from the statuette, the light vanished and in its place, was a solid gold, sparkling image of the

Goddess Durga. The earthen gold-bordered statue had transmuted into a solid gold one. He gave it to me and my dream ended.

When they opened the first chapter of my Naadi it said the words: 'YOU WILL GREATLY BENEFIT IF YOU PRAY TO GODDESS DURGA.' The Durga He produced in my dream darshan and the message I got from my reading confirmed (in my mind), that His consent was there and He told me, in essence, the message the Universe was giving me. I believe this was His affirmation."

Anu sent me the transcripts of her family readings that are too long to reproduce here but I found her 89 year old father's reading fascinating and I think it must have been comforting for a man who was approaching the end of his days. It said "You have age related problems. You hardly walk," which was true as he's had a series of cerebral attacks over the last three years, which had affected the parts of his brain relating to mobility. The MCA and PCA regions on both sides of the brain had serious problems. The leaf also described how they had lost the thumbprint for her father but found it again. The leaf explained that this happened because this was the time ordained by Agashthya Maharishi to find and open the oracle.

"The Naadi wrote that my grandfather was part of a 'famous family'," says Anu "this is a remarkable point for I come from a famous family of landowners in West Bengal. My father's side has a recorded family history, written by a historian researching the famous families of Howrah, which dates back to more than 650 years. My paternal grandfather was very advanced in his thinking and a true feminist. He was the founder President of all the institutions, schools and colleges promoting women's education in Howrah. He was a double MA in Physics and Philosophy more than 130 years ago."

The Naadi also saw her father's inability to communicate because of his illness: "You are in a situation where you are unable to express some of your thoughts," it said – the poor man had had a major cerebral attack that was making speech difficult. It explained that he'd wanted to outlive everyone in his previous life and his illness now was part of the karmic cost. "This is why Agashthya Maharishi wrote your leaf a few years before you're due to expire, so that you do not experience any pain at the time of leaving, so that there is no residual karma when you leave and so that there are no regrets. If these remedies are carried out, you will have a good birth in your next life.

You will be born into a good life without any problems in your arm/legs."

Anu tells me that her father had broken his arm a number of times but within, 10 days of his Gurudaan Pujas being performed, her father not only became fully lucid but could move his arm properly for the first time in years. Rada says: "Daddy's first action was to raise his hand and bless me. He was overjoyed to be able to caress my cheek after I hugged him."

It concluded with a hopeful message for a better life in the next world and future incarnation. "In the afternoon, when your wife, daughter and grandson will be by your side, you will become like a new born child. All your activities will be become like a newborn child. You will gradually lose your memory. You will feel your predeceased relatives calling you. You will be able to get a Darshan of the form of God you worshipped. You will feel as though you're falling asleep when your soul leaves your body. You have one more life on earth and you will be born as a male without any health problems into a family of very high position and status."

Anu was inspired by the Naadi's remedies and insights and it brings it home to her how lucky she has been to be born into such a family. "I feel that my father is on the verge of liberation. He's an incredibly loving person and his love and protection of me is like folklore amongst everyone who knows him. Even though I know attachment is an obstacle to spiritual advancement and liberation, I still pray that he'll be my dad in my next life and I want my mum too! I've been incredibly lucky to be born to the parents I've been born to and I'll go to any lengths for their happiness, peace, comfort and anything else any parent might need or want."

Later, in a message on Facebook, Anu explained what happened when the remedies were completed. She had been told by the oracle, that her father was on the verge of Moksha (liberation at death) and a special talisman had been made to help him in the short term and free him at death. The Naadi reader was very excited as this was only the second person who had been given a Jeeva Shanthi Moksha talisman in eight years. Her father was a man who had never transgressed from the path of Truth so full realization was near. Once the mantras were complete, she took the talisman to her father:

"Well, for a man who was barely conscious last evening, he's started walking with minimal support this morning within 3 hours of putting on the Jeeva Shanti Moksha Tabeej. It's TRULY like seeing Sai Baba holding someone's hand, raising them from the wheelchair and making them walk. And I'm getting a LIVE show with my Daddy being held by God's invisible hand. I was feeling so emotional while putting the talisman on him Craig. I love him so much, yet here I was, cutting the ties that bind by my own hand, through my own efforts, knowing that it would be for his ultimate good. It makes me feel choked up and teary. Later I asked him what he was thinking about and he repeated the exact same words that were written in the oracle."

The more readings I witness close hand, the more I am convinced of the authenticity of the Naadi oracles. I'm sure some reader must think that I have become intoxicated by this whole India thing and, perhaps, even taken in by the flattering messages, which I've had from the Naadis. I've introduced others to the oracles that I've just mentioned above and, every time, I am startled to hear of the exact information they have to say about the sitter's life – very personal details that no one else could possibly know or look up on the Internet or Facebook.

Learning how to read the leaves for myself

In India I'd had the chance to handle the leaves and Mr. Prakash had given me some simple lessons in reading the leaves. You don't have to be clairvoyant to do this as it's simply a matter of reading the predictions and remedies that were written in these leaves thousands of years ago. Carbon dating shows the leaves to be about 500 years old but the claim is that they have been copied and recopied hundreds of times over many thousands of years.

Mr. Prakash chants the Tamil text of the leaves and then shows me what it says word by word. He does this with a leaf that is randomly selected from the pile. The first leaf is often the most interesting as, in the first few lines, they usually contain the names and family names of the people who will consult the leaves. It is clear, as the words are translated one-by-one, that there is not much room for improvisation or cold reading. I remain in awe of what is written and fascinated by what strange things will be revealed to others who consult this pile of old palm leaves.

As a typical westerner visiting India I feel conscious that I have come from a country of great materialism and comforts where spirituality has been lost and is now replaced by rampant rationality. If India's temples crumbled to dust and its teachings were ever lost, how poorer still would the world become. The writing is on the wall: we all know that the world is heading towards catastrophe if we do not change our ways and perhaps these Naadi teachings are there to help us put a break on materialism and to rediscover a spiritual heritage that's there for everyone, no matter what your religion or nationality.

The Promethean fires still burn and the lost knowledge of the ancients is still there for us to discover. Treading where holy men have walked reminds me that this has been an inner journey. My destiny has been predicted and I have been helped by the astrologers and their teachings to understand better the reason I have been placed upon this earth.

The teachings are as old as the hills. The oracle that inspired me is thousands of years old and yet there is nothing really new. It's the same journey we take now as the ancients had to take. We just need to have the courage to open into the divinity within us. In every face I've seen in India is a little of that divine light that India's teachings take us towards. Spiritual teachings are not just something remote but are anchored in everyday life, in the things we do. There can be worship even in the simplest of work.

We are all evolving, not just as physical beings but spiritually too. The teachings tell us that our soul has evolved from animal into human and our time on earth now in human form is an opportunity to become fully awakened. And that's why so many take to the spiritual path, touch the feel of gurus or seek the solace of meditation.

I have thrown myself into mystic India and undertaken rituals that many would find perplexing. I have had the blessings of the gods and of holy people and holy places and have done many rituals to open the path that the oracle predicts will happen. Some of this has been a cultural shock but I feel that it is leading me to the light. My adventure has taken me thousands of miles across India and I have enjoyed places that few westerners visit.

But it has taught me, also, the importance of charity. As we give to others, their good thoughts, projected towards us, help us to evolve, too. It's a win-win situation. And, of course, helping others is a part of the Christian message, too, and the Muslim message, and the Buddhist and Jewish message... I think I have learned that there is not much difference between it all. It's an adventure doing spiritual things and, when people really get helped and you see their lives quickly changed, it opens your heart wide.

Will all these strange astrological remedies change things? I have done the rituals and I have burnt the karma; I have thrown the past into the flames. I have taken my journey and explored my soul. I have cut the ties with my karma and now a new destiny awaits.

CHAPTER 18

ॐ

Heaven and Reincarnation

My work as a medium has been greatly influenced by Spiritualism, which, for people in the UK, was for many years the only place they could see us mediums working. I was illegal to practice as a medium until 1951 and only in recent years has it been allowed on UK television so long as it is screened as 'entertainment'. On mainstream television, the Broadcasting Codes continue to put mediumship under the 'occult' category and demonstrations of mediumship are usually vigorously challenged by sceptics and psychologists or ridiculed by comedians and conjurers. I find it hard to work out why 'dabbling in religion' isn't the same as 'dabbling in the occult'. Having unsubstantiated beliefs is fine but proving the reality of spirit is dangerous.

Fortunately, spiritual censorship is not as bad as it was and, today, you can watch mediums on cable, Internet and satellite television, listen to readings on late night radio, see mediums at the theatre, call for a personal consultation by phone or even watch them demonstrating at pubs. The snag is that, now mediumship has moved outside of Spiritualism, it means that anyone can claim to be a medium without ever having sat in a development circle or practised on a Spiritualist rostrum. Standards have slipped and some of the material that passes off as spirit communication is shameful and sometimes frightening.

One of the seven principles of Spiritualism is the simple phrase 'personal responsibility'. From a philosophical standpoint, this is the idea that we choose, instigate, or otherwise cause our own actions. In other words we have free will and are, therefore, morally responsible for the results of our actions. The official Spiritualist National Union explanation of the principle of 'personal responsibility' that was given by the spirit world through the trance and table séances of the medium Emma Hardinge Britten (1823 – 1899) is described thus: "In His wisdom, God has given us enormous potential; we can use that potential to improve our own lives and the lives of others. We have the ability to make decisions throughout our lives as we see fit. What each of us makes of our life is our Personal Responsibility; no one can replace or override that right. No other person or influence can put right our wrong doings."

I take this to mean that we accept our karma and are prepared to live out the consequences. I would personally remove the references to God as the same principle could be relevant to someone with atheist views or a non-dualist like me who does not necessarily believe in a Creator God that is in any way separate from our own divinity.

Mediums who have never worked within Spiritualism may not be aware of this fundamental principle that is so important to take into consideration when giving readings or messages from the spirit world. If we have free will, as this spirit teaching implies, then the future is not set, as we can change it though our own will. This is also why mediums working within Spiritualism are told never to make predictions, for to tell the future would undermine the principle of 'personal responsibility' and, with it, free will.

Most Spiritualists would argue that making predictions is unhelpful as it may disempower the recipient of the spirit message and disrupt their ability to make their own choices. From a practical point of view this also stops less experienced mediums from making frightening predictions or giving advice about unavoidable calamity. Mediums limit themselves to giving evidence of survival and comforting messages from the spirit that sometimes give wise advice about the best way to act but never predict an unalterable future. The sad fact is that many of the 'mediums' who have stormed the media and internet today have not even thought about these ideas and, in many cases, don't even realize the difference between low level psychic sensing and real messages from the spirit.

Clearly the guidance of Spiritualism, and in particular its focus on personal responsibility and free will, can help to protect people who are genuinely seeking to know about the reality of the spirit world. The simple safeguards I have described act as a protection from wild mediumship, daft fantasy and misguided psychism. The fact is that people seeking predictions do not really want to know the future but simply want to know that the future is going to be all right and in accordance with their hopes. They want a reassurance and a prop.

In my mediumistic work I will not make predictions for the reasons I've mentioned and I feel it is important to keep focused on proof of survival and not be distracted by other issues. Nonetheless this does not mean that it is impossible to see the future. It may be the case that the spirit people are also subject to similar rules of karma and, by being so entwined, may not be able to see their own destiny and future Earthly incarnations.

Squaring many of the ideas found in Indian philosophies with my own spiritualist work as a psychic medium can sometimes be difficult. As a medium I endeavor to prove, through evidence given from a spirit communicator, that life continues after death. By proving that the personality and memories survive death am I not also proving the existence of a soul? Immediately this conflicts with the Buddhist belief that asserts that there is no soul. This is also a fundamental difference between Hinduism and Buddhism, which was explained by the Hindu philosopher and theologian Adi Shankara (788 CE – 820 CE), who said that the key difference between Hinduism and Buddhism is that "Atman (Soul, Self) exists", whereas Buddhism asserts that there is "no Soul, no Self".

Today the biggest disparity is between the materialistic model of the world and the spiritual model. The extremist materialist doesn't believe in anything beyond the material world, dismisses God, religion and mediumship as foolish beliefs and focuses on making best use of the present worldly life through science, engineering, politics and so on. For moral values he may draw upon philosophy and reasoned arguments. In contrast, the spiritual extremist sees the world as the creation of the deceitful *maya* (illusion) and the only true reality is the eternal, infinite Brahma (Spirit) that is beyond duality and is without form and void. At this extreme the goal is to renounce the world and escape material existence entirely and eventually to become one with the formless infinite and – in a way – be no more.

Some Eastern teachers regard the world as something imperfect and taught people they should focus entirely on escaping the world. Meanwhile, in the West, with the growth of extreme materialism, religion becomes the butt of jokes and an activity done by old ladies as a sort of hobby, or by mixed-up people looking to hide from themselves. The task of religion is to awaken the consciousness, embrace the truth, pop the bubble of illusion and educate the world towards the values tolerance and peace. Its aim is not to run away from your fears, inadequacies or from your very existence. In the religious extremes, which reject the world, it seems to me that the soul is the victim by being denied its purpose and growth.

Whatever way you look at it, earthly life is full of suffering so long as we are isolated from our divine nature. The remedy is to seek union with our divine, higher self and become one with the will of the Universe – some may call this God's will. Simultaneously we will enthusiastically engage in worldly life, not reject the outer would and try to hide in Brahma/Nirvana, and even do the terrible work of war if this serves the divine purpose. Life is one with spirit. We can live for life's sake, giving up the fruits of our actions and expecting no personal reward, knowing only that our will is at one with the divine. This is what Krishna taught the confused Arjuna on the battlefield of Kurukshetra and is the essence of the Vedas culture found in the Upanishads and the Gita.

Doing the remedies taught me that every soul is a shining light which is cloaked by our past misdeeds from previous lives. This is the same for all people, for nobody is a sinner; all we have done is simply to mask our inner pure light with our misdeeds. Nothing can change the quality of the soul for it is pure and eternal but, by following a good and moral life, we can rediscover our innate inner divinity. Wicked actions bring negative karma that mask the light and keep us away from the bliss and joy that lies at the heart of our being but, no matter what we have done to draw the veil over the indestructible soul, we can, with work, rediscover our hidden divinity.

By freeing ourselves of our past karma through spiritual work and sincere and devotional ritual practice, we begin to free the soul from the shackles of illusion so that it can find its purpose here on earth and flower in the inner light. Sometimes doubts, like a virus, will infect our faith but we will grow spiritually stronger as the inner person grows at the expense of outward yearning. With persistent spiritual practice we become a pure vessel and with this comes great intuitive power that is unsullied by fantasy or uncertainty. As doubt and hesitancy continue to fall away, this intuition becomes pure and free of personal thought and a way to direct knowledge of reality.

Free of the fluctuations of thought, the ultimate intuition reveals itself as no-mind, as the knower of Brahman and of being Brahman itself.

These ideas do not in, my opinion, conflict with the core ideas within spiritualist philosophy. As mediums we are taught that there is an eternal progress of the human soul so, in effect, the Spiritualists subscribe to the idea that spiritual evolution and the soul go on forever after earthly life. In the UK, Spiritualists do not generally accept reincarnation as a fact, citing that, unlike proof of the afterlife, there is not enough evidence to accept it as fact. Some reject the idea on the basis that it was not included in the 'Seven Principles of Spiritualism' that were allegedly dictated by the spirit people through the mediumship of Emma Hardinge Britten and were later adopted as the fundamental basis of Spiritualist philosophy at the National Spiritualist Conference in 1890. Emma Hardinge Britten's view was that Spiritualism is threatened if it admits theoretical speculations about reincarnation that are not supported by evidence. She even called the reincarnation a "fungus on Spiritualism."

Emma Hardinge Britten strikes me as a somewhat opinioned spirit channel and her own thoughts and prejudices may have influenced the alleged spirit communications. I consider Spiritualism's early rejection of reincarnation a big mistake that is contributing to the gradual demise of the movement today. Despite this, many mediums accept reincarnation as a fact and, although talk of it is still suppressed during addresses from the rostrum, we can nowadays find our own platforms on YouTube and other social media to express these ideas.

Today I rarely give addresses at Spiritualist churches. What I now see passing off as philosophy is frankly banal rubbish based on wooly thinking and the silly fantasies of little old ladies who do 'mediumship' as a hobby. Sadly, there are now very few powerful spiritualist speakers or mediums working in what's left of the Spiritualist Churches. It is a very sad situation despite the fact that there is today a huge public hunger for all things paranormal. This is what happens when religious movements become bogged down in intractable beliefs and spiritual complacency.

Perhaps if Emma Hardinge Britten were alive today her opinions may have been swayed by the accumulating evidence for reincarnation published by researchers such as Professor Ian Stevenson, Dr Erlendur Haraldsson, Jürgen Keil and Dr Satwant Pasricha. In her own time other mediums were saying that reincarnation should be part of a medium's message. Allan Kardec in France, who compiled *The Spirits' Book*, built the theories of reincarnation into French Spiritism's philosophy and, after the First World War, reincarnation philosophy was imparted by a number of British trance mediums, whose guides included Silver Birch, Red Cloud and White Eagle.

As you have read in this book, I consider reincarnation to be a fact and that the karma generated from our past life activities influences this life, the life in spirit and our future incarnations on earth. I ask people who accept mediumship as a fact to further broaden their views and think more deeply about the purpose of human life on earth and in the next world. Mediumship is a wonderful thing that can prove to us that we do not need to fear death and that life will go on afterwards, first in the spirit world and then again later in new earthly lives, but all this good news should not make us complacent for we are given these opportunities so that we can seek out the meaning and purpose of life and death. If we fail to do this we will, again, fall deep into the delusion of Maya with its cycles of suffering and rebirth. The afterlife is not an escape.

In India there are holy men who are also mediums but, unlike in Britain and America, there are few opportunities for the common man to experience mediumship directly. This is one of the precious teachings that we can share with the east, just as we can learn so much from them too.

Although there are many schools of thought within Hinduism there are many core facts about the afterlife that correspond closely with Spiritualist teachings. Western spirituality mostly believes in the existence of an individual soul. This soul is what the Indians call the *jivatman* that in turn is part of the *paramatman* which is the Universal Soul that is practically identical to Brahman (God) in a state of *saccidananda* (Existence Consciousness Bliss). The goal of our life is to realize the unity of the two, that we are in fact God finding expression through many souls. This is not an intellectual or an emotional realization but involves the totality of what we are. The *jivatman* becomes one with the *paramatma*, our spark of divinity merges with the great ocean of divinity and bliss. This union is called

Yoga.

At death, the individual sheds its human body like a worn out garment and is carried in the subtle body sheath that houses the *jivatman*. We are, in effect, now moving around in our spiritual underwear in the astral planes. Nearly all individuals enter these astral planes after death where they work out the seeds of past karma through astral incarnations. In these astral realms called *Hiranya loka* the discarnate soul reaps the harvest of earthly life acts, which were done with expectation of reward or punishment. Eventually the soul may return to earthly incarnations once the propelling force of good karma is exhausted and so that the spirit may be further refined. The soul continues to move between these different blissful planes in the afterlife until it evolves enough to become free of the chain of cause (desire) and effect (births) and attains the highest liberated state of spiritual knowledge which is *nirvikalpa samadhi* – the total oneness, transcendental silence and boundless peace of permanent God Realization.

My and Jane's work as mediums gives people comforting proof of the continuation of life after death and the glorious world of spirit that awaits us on the other shore. I hope my experience of India has also helped you to understand the bigger picture and how life here on earth is a mystical journey from here and into the beyond that is fueled by our past karma.

Nothing ever dies. Our soul survives death and so, too, do our thoughts and deeds. They fly from us as if on wings to create new opportunities or obstacles in our future. If our thoughts, feelings and actions are filled with love, forgiveness and compassion, they become holy remedies that will transform our destiny into a path of endless joy.

APPENDIX

I have included some of my most relevant Naadi readings so that you can read exactly what was said and compare it with the appendix of my book *Messages from the Universe*.

What follows are the Kandams (Chapters) that are opened after the initial leaf finding process that gives my name and the names of my family and so on. You can read mind-boggling examples of these in the appendix of my first book. You can also cross-reference the predictions and things said here with the examples in my other book.

Publishing these, often personal things, about my life and future serve as a proof – or otherwise – of the Naadi. In years to come, and maybe after I'm dead, I hope it may serve as a useful resource to people in the future who wish to research this remarkable oracle.

Gnana Kandam Naadi Reading

This is the full transcript of the Gnana Kandam sent to me by audio file. (Vivek's Reader)

[Tape 1]
Namaste. Om shri Nagasdaya Namaha. On Nama Shivaya.

May the blessings of Sat Guru Sri Agurum shower on the native. The Gnana Kandam of Mr. Craig is being explained by Naadi astrologer Mr V R Shiva Shakti.

Lord Shiva, who is in the form of Amodum or Amrithum, or the fluid or the form of energy which was absorbed by gods and goddesses to become immortal in the heavens and Lord Shiva who is in the form of happiness and pleasure and Lord Shiva who is in the form of five elements and who is praised and prayed and worshiped by the people of the Universe and Lord Shiva who performs the divine dance in the heaven with goddess Parvati and who performs the dance with divine anger and who danced to suppress the arrogance of goddess Parvati and stretched one of his legs towards the sky while dancing. Such Lord Shiva explains the Gnana Kandam of the native Mr. Craig.

The Hindi people have a custom of praying to God before starting doing anything. Like that, goddess Parvati prays to Lord Shiva who is in the form of five elements. Ahodum, or Amrithum, is a fluid which was extracted from Filpalkulum – that is divine ocean of divine milk. It was extracted with the help of a hill named Mandarah and a snake named Vasaghi which was used as a rope to still the ocean of divine milk to extract the Amrithum.

Before extracting the fluid named Amrithum, first poison came out. Lord Shiva drank the poison to save all god and goddesses and the saints who live in the heaven. Lord Shiva also guided the saints who guided the people in the world to lead their life peacefully with happiness. Lord Shiva who gave the spiritual knowledge to the people of the world. Lord Shiva shovels the knowledge of spirituality and the knowledge of something beyond the worldly life. Lord Shiva shovels the spiritual knowledge and spiritual energy on the native.

Lord Shiva explains the time period when the native is going to get the spiritual knowledge and the other knowledges beyond the worldly life and the knowledge of divine life and when the native is going to get matured to get this knowledge and sustain this knowledge and from whom the native is going to get this knowledge or Gnanam. And after getting this Gnanam what are the changes the native is going to experience in his divine life.

Lord Shiva is very much pleased to explain the Gnana Kandam of the native. After getting Gnanam, the native is going to serve the world in many ways and help many people in many ways. The native will have more spiritual powers and more mental powers. The native will get good name and fame after getting the Gnanam. The native is a child of Lord Shiva and goddess Parvati. With the blessings of Lord Shiva and goddess Parvati the native is going to get Gnanam and after getting this Gnana he is going to serve many people and he will be having spiritual powers more than a saint and he will be praised almost as God.

The native has good luck to serve many people, save many people and guide many people to lead their life on the way of happiness, peace and spirituality. Lord Shiva feels happy in explaining Gnana Kandam because a human is going to get Gnanam and will almost become a god and save many people. Almost become a god and save many people of the world and guide them.

And to get this Gnanam and to use this Gnanam for the welfare of the world a level of maturity is necessary. For that the native has to follow certain things to get the maturity and to use the spiritual powers for the welfare of the world the native has to follow certain things in his life. He has to cultivate morality.

When Lord Shiva is explaining these things, Shiva Vakyaha Maharishi is writing this on a palm leaf. Gnana Kandam is a chapter which not everyone can get. It's very rare. A person can get Gnana Kandam only after reaching a certain level in spirituality. The native is very lucky in this way so the native has got his Gnana Kandam.

There are certain things written in this palm leaf which prove that this Gnana Kandam is written for the native. The native's birth ascendant is Libra. The birth star of the native is Hasta. The moon sign is Virgo. The native's name is Craig. Donald is his father's name and Ethel is his mother's name. When the native is listening to this chapter his age is 62.

All these things prove that this chapter belongs to the native. The things that the native has to follow before getting the Gnanam and how the native's life will be after he gets the Gnanam. All these things are being explained.

In the present period the native will get the blessings of saints. Gnanam is a divine power beyond the powers of human beings. At present the native is learning and practising spirituality. He is also learning the theories of spirituality himself. He has to learn a few arts related to spirituality. He need not learn anything modern. All the things he has to learn are ancient. All plants and animals are blessed by God so because of this they perish themselves and save the people of the world. So Gnanam is something to devote ourselves for the welfare and wellbeing of the people of the world.

The native has the talent to learn anything very soon. The native will learn the arts related to spirituality very soon for example yoga, meditation, Homa, the theories related to spirituality that is chakras. He will learn most everything he will learn almost every true thing related to spirituality.

Before getting the Gnanam the native must have got success in leading his family life. Being in family life the native will learn the things related to spirituality and develop himself. And his knowledge will be expressed outside now and then. The native will become famous because of his spiritual knowledge.

After getting success in his family life, the native will serve people and guide many people. The native will solve the problems of people and he will be able to give happiness to people. After that the native will lead his life as a saint.

The native will use his knowledge of curing people using spirituality – that is healing. The native will know the secrets to cure many chronic diseases. Also the native will teach many secrets to many people which were not revealed till that time and by knowing these secrets, the people will be able to cure their diseases and even the diseases of other people. Then the native can lead his life according to his wish.

The native will do some pujas himself and also he will do some virtuous deeds and serve people and the world.

The native has to keep a Shiva Lingam and worship it. Shiva Lingam is the symbolism of both male and female together. The native should also keep the photograph of the person whom the person thinks as his own guru and worship him. And also the native should do pilgrimage and worship various gods and goddesses. The native has to learn a few Mulah Mantras from gurus and the native has to chant those mantras daily. The native has to learn the secrets of the Sashtras – that is the ancient theories of spirituality.

In between the native's 62 and 63 the native has the chance to do pilgrimage and get the blessings of gods and goddesses. The native will get the blessings of gods and goddesses through nature, for example the five elements which are the nature in whole. By worshiping the five elements the native will get the blessings of God. And also the native should worship everything which he sees through his eyes.

In the month when the Sun transits to its enemy's house – that is Vygasi month according to the Tamil almanac, that is between May and June of English calendar, the native will learn the art of curing the diseases of people using spirituality. The native will, and has to, learn this art without a guru. He has to learn this art himself.

He has to go to some gurus to learn a few things but you have to practice yourself in the absence of that guru. So for doing anything or practising anything you will not be having a guru with you. Occasionally the native will be getting a few gurus but no guru will be permanent for the native.

[Tape 2]

The native will be a person who cures many people's diseases, who cures the problems of many people and who fulfils the needs of many people. Because of the native's guidance, many people will be leading their life with happiness and peace. Many people will bless and praise the native. When the people will lead their life with happiness and peace, they wholeheartedly will bless and praise the native. There is development in the native's life because of the blessings of these people.

The native will solve the problems of many people, will solve the confusions in the minds of many people and will fulfil the needs of many people. The native can help many people to know their future and get eradicated from the bad effects of the sins they had committed in their past lives. And also the methods to get rid of the bad effects of black magic, the bad vision of bad people envy and conspiracy of bad people by knowing their future and remedial measures chapters from the Naadi Shastras. The native will do some consultation related to this. The native will do this as a social service.

The native will teach many arts to many people. He will preach Gnanam to many people — that is spiritual knowledge to many people. The native will teach many arts to many people. He will preach Gnanam to many people. In the age of 63 in the Vaikasi masum — that is the month between May and June — the native has to start practising a few things. He has to wake up in the early morning time, the time when the animals start waking up, that is between 4.30am and 6.00am he has to wake up and take bath. He has to sit and meditate as a sanyasi — that is being cut off from the family life and the worldly life. The native has to sit and meditate. He has to meditate for almost one and a half hours that is from 4.30 am to 6.00 am and he has to continue this for three mandalas that is 144 days.

The native has to chant mantras and he has to worship Lord Shiva. By doing this the native slowly takes his steps towards maturity to get the Gnanam — that is the spiritual knowledge. After doing this meditation the native has to feed cows or bulls. The native will get blessings from a guru who is born in a country far away from the native's country. And the guru will be much younger than the native. The guru will be a Hindu and a person who will be worshiping Lord Shiva.

After getting his blessings there are a few changes, a few good changes, in the native's life. There will be some good changes inside the body as well as in the mind of the native.

In 64 and 65 the native will meet a person, a guru, who much younger than him but he looks mature and old and who has learned many arts related to spirituality. By getting the blessings and advice of this guru there are a few changes, good changes, in the life of the native.

In this period the native will meet a person who looks almost like a beggar. The person will not have anyone to support. The person will be staying somewhere near the temple of Lord Shiva, goddess Parvati or Lord Ganesha or Lord Murgan. The person's name will be the name of an incarnation of Lord Shiva. The person will be a male. By seeing him, the native will automatically raise both his hands and he will start worshiping that person.

After that, the person will give some blessings to the native. After giving blessings to the native, the person will disappear within a few moments. So before getting the Gnanam, the native has to help many people to know their future as well as the remedial measures through the palm leaf inscriptions written by Shiva Vatyah Maharishi. So by doing this the native helps many people to get eradicated from the problems due to their previous birth sins, bad effects of bad vision, envy, conspiracy, black magic, etcetera, and he serves many people and many people will give blessings to the native and because of this the native will become more and more matured to sustain the unlimited spiritual power and he will be able to help many people directly by solving their problems, by curing their chronic diseases and by sharing his knowledge, his spiritual knowledge, for many people.

The native will also get blessings from the people who lead their life almost like prostitutes and also from the people who have both the genders inside themselves. He will get blessings from those people. The native will meet such people when he is travelling. The native will donate some coins to those people and get blessings from them. The name of these people will be related to a planet.

In the age of 66 when the sun is in the Nijasplanner? – that is Puraṭṭasi month according to Tamil almanac – the native will be matured enough to get the unlimited spiritual knowledge. That is Gnanam. According to English calendar it is between September and October. In this period the native will get the blessings of a person who has both femaleness and maleness in their body and they are actually, that is the person is actually Lord Shiva and goddess Parvati. They are not actually human but gods who come on earth to bless the native. The native will meet that person, that is actually Lord Shiva and goddess Parvati on the day of Agranatchatra – that is isvarar? star. This is the star of Lord Shiva. The person will bless the native and soon disappear. The native can't meet this person once again in this birth or any birth in the future.

After getting the blessing from this person the native will get the Gnanam. The native will use all the arts related to spirituality and he will use all these arts practically and get success in every task he does to serve people and the world. Then a person comes to the native with a problem; the native, without asking them anything about their problem, the native himself comes to know about the problems with his spiritual knowledge and explains clearly about the problem and he will solve the problem easily with his spiritual powers.

The native's spiritual eye will be open – that is the third eye will be open. Even when the native closes his eyes he will be able to know everything around him through his spiritual eye. When the native closes his eyes he will be able to see the rays of gods and goddesses.

The native will be able to meditate on his third eye. The native will have echasity? – that is whatever he thinks he will be able to execute it and echasity is whatever he thinks it happens naturally and kriya Shakti – that is whatever he thinks he wants to do he can execute it and get success in that. He will also have Gnana Shakti – that is the power to get knowledge of anything he wants.

The native will learn nearly all the arts related to spirituality and in 67 the native will start teaching and preaching spirituality to many people. He will be able to predict the natural calamities and, by predicting this, he will be helping many people to go to safer places before the calamities.

The native will have enough knowledge about Yantra, Mantra and Sashtra – that is the ancient theories of spirituality. Till the end the native will lead his life for the welfare and wellbeing of the people.

The native will do pilgrimage; he will travel to a few countries and pray to gods and goddesses. He will be able to serve the people of other countries also. The native will become very famous in the field of spirituality. He will be able to build a temple. The native will worship his guru and Lord Shiva. The native will also build an ashram and he will be the guru in that ashram. The native will get enough spiritual knowledge – that is Gnanam – and will live a life of high status. In this period the native will keep a Shiva Lingam and worship it.

The native will be able to predict the natural calamities related to water, earth, fire or wind and will save the lives of many people by helping them to go to safer places before the natural calamities attack the people.

The native will also be able to do powerful pujas which can prevent the natural calamities.

In 68, 69, 70 the native will be teaching many spiritual lessons to many people. In his old age the native will be very much active like a young man. The native will be mature enough to use the spiritual powers. His mind will be clear. He will be clear about what he is going to do next.

After 67 the native will lead his life using his Gnanam – that is spiritual knowledge. The native will lead his life which is not normal and which is something beyond the life of a human. That is for 14 hours the native will lead his life as a human and for ten hours the native will lead his life with divineness. That is he will lead his life almost like a god. Like that by giving a lot of blessings Shiva concludes the Gnana Kandam of the native and Shiva Vakiya Maharishi completes this chapter with a lot of blessings. Thankyou. Shupam. Namaste.

Brahma Sukshma Naadi
– BRAHMA MAHARISHI

BIRTH DETAILS

First Brahma Maharishi prays to Lord Ganesh, Lord Hanuman and Lord Shiva and his consort Parvathi. This to enable the Maharishi and the reader to perform his utmost best to convey the inner and external message to this seeker, whom by now it is seen, is ready to hear these our words and guidance for a happy and blessed life and enable him to see and understand about his true spiritual purpose of life and beyond. It is only after some obstacles in his life it has been possible for him to have this and some other few readings.

Brahma Maharishi speaks now:

This child is born in the Tamil year Vijaya, in the month Thai, on the 11th day, corresponding to the English date January 24st 1954, on a Sunday, during the night hours. His Moon is in Virgo in Uttira star and his rising sign is in Libra.
From his rising sign it is seen that Mars and Saturn are there; in his 4th house is 4 planets. Raghu is there but he is also in the previous sign Sagittarius and, with this, he is having a double effect. The other planets there are Venus, Sun and Mercury. In his 8th house is Jupiter in his Vak movements – retrograde so he will also act as being in 2 signs i.e., in Taurus as well as Aries. The spiritual planet and Gnana karaka Kethu in his 10th house and Moon in his 12th house.
From his Moon in Virgo, Mars and Saturn is in the 2nd, Sun, Mercury, Venus and Rahu in 5th house. Jupiter in 9th house and Ketu in 11th house. So looking into both, it is shown that he will have much power and support from Moon in his 12th house, 4 meaning also that he will be able to achieve much recognition, respect and fame outside his birth place.
He has several auspicious combinations and Yogas. But also Mars and Saturn in his rising sign. Libra will make him overcome many of the obstacles coming during his life. This combination will also, in

the beginning of his life, show a very self-opined person with some temper but later, as he matures, show much insight and knowledge taking him wide and high in the world and on the path towards deep and profound spiritual knowledge.

Looking in to the planetary movements both from his Rasi/Moon and rising sign, it is seen that he will be greatly benefitted by foreign contacts and some foreign gurus and highly evolved spiritual beings on his path to know more about himself.

His thumb impression is called Suzhi Sangu Kalasa Rekha and there are 4 dots within that. So he will be able to handle multiple tasks at the same time and always he will seek higher and higher aspirations for his move and development in life. 5

In general he is a lucky man. He will be very eager to know more and more about new as well as old things. He is very eager to manifest or convey important messages to the world. He will at the same time possess great administrative power and he will, as years goes by, year by year, more and more, come to see his ideas and wishes come true. In the beginning of his life his focus will be a mixture of much curiosity and excitement and, later on, a more developed and deeper spiritual approach to understand his own ways of pattern and interests and finally being able to free himself from unnecessary concern of what is, and what is not, important in life and beyond. We see much good promises for this blessed person.

PREDICTIONS FOR THE PERIOD OF HIS 62 – 70TH RUNNING YEARS.

1. During the period of his 62 – 65th running years, he needs to take more care in his life. Some sudden changes will come and he will have to face some place of transfer. He will travel here and there, sometimes having doubts about his moves. He may have to face some unwanted bad names and less respect in his life. He will face some unwanted problems and conflicts. There will be some physical issues to his mother. Through this his mother will face some medical expenses. There may be some unexpected risk of involvement in a vehicle accident; however nothing will come to harm him. Overall this is a turning point in his life, saying goodbye to patterns and ideas of no validity any more, as well as persons close to him.

2. There may be some conflicts in his family. Especially Brahma Maharishi is mentioning that his daughters may come to face some problems in their family life.

3. There may be some theft to him or in his family. There may be some financial issues and losses and simply high expenses. It will not always be easy for him to keep his mind at peace. Some worries will come and go and he do better not to put too much attention to such worries but leave it all to his spiritual guide and see it as a process of maturing his mind. His mother will be in bed rest and she may pass away in this period.

4. His sleep will at time be disturbed and sometimes he will not have a good sleep. He will have to confront and possess some mental disturbances in his life. Brahma Maharishi says that all these karmic results are all happenings caused by himself in his past life. It is better for him to follow the advices and suggestions from the Maharishis to overcome and minimize the past karmic effect and to lead a happy life. He will face some negative events in this life because of the past karmic effect. After performing the suggested puja advices, he and his daughters will possess a good life.

1. Because of his Punya – good deeds in some previous lifetime – then he is already in the process of following the Maharishis, so he himself will develop a higher spiritual approach and knowledge to possess a spiritual-related consultancy/advice business on a very high level, by which he will achieve much honor and respect in the world. He will also develop and possess good contacts with spiritual persons and gain much from this on several levels.

2. Brahma Maharishi is saying that this gentle person will get a special blessed spiritual advisor. And this will happen all of a sudden but also that the spiritual advisor, not at first, will let him come to know about his ways. This child here will have to find out about his whereabouts for himself and who he is. When the time is ready he will know.

He will have interest and knowledge of several spiritual beings and masters and he will take from them freely what he feels is in accordance with his inner understanding and knowledge. He will have peaceful situations in his family life. He will possess all the good chances to get and develop many new contacts in his life.

He will get some good benefits through the Government as well as VIP persons also. He will be respected by the public and be able to stand up in front of many people and convey his message. He will face a good development in life. He will have the grace and blessings (Visions) from God in his dreams. And he should cherish such dreams and not share such things with all people but better keep it to himself.

9. He will get business assistants in his life. He will get income without any obstacle. His will possess many a good opportunities to travel to other countries. His children will have a good family life. He will come to have a very close relationship with his grandchildren. During this period he will possess some digestion problems, but it will be minimized by some simple yoga postures/exercises. This gentleman is born to share, convey and fulfil himself in this generation through the spiritual events and deep spirituality overall.

PREDICTIONS FOR THE PERIOD OF HIS 71 – 79TH YEARS RUNNING.

1. During this period he will work hard. He will continue to have high administrative power. His siblings will live in different places but they will have a close relationship. His grandchildren will have a good education. The persons who did not respect or deal with him in a kind way before, will come and surrender to him and seek to be helpful with his activities. He will get assistance from his family members on a good level, too.

2. He will follow some daily spiritual exercises. By following this he will have a good physique and health. He will be benefitted and blessed by his spiritual advisor, sometimes even though he is not fully aware of this. He will have a peaceful mind and also he will have a good health. He will have all such blessings from Brahma Maharishi also. Through this he will have more properties such as house, vehicle, rental buildings, etc. His children's life will be good in this period but also later on in their future.

3. He will have a good mutual understanding with his siblings, wife and children. During this period however he will also for some time have a physical issues such as tiredness and weakness etc. But this will be minimized through the medical herbal treatments and with Brahma Maharishi and God's grace.

4. The above said good events will happen in his life because he have and is already engaged in some remedial measures while hearing these my words of minimizing his past karmic effect.

5. He will write an autobiography book and he will release this book in this period. He will also set up an ashram-like institution in this period. And he will prefer to stay as much as possible there in this ashram and he will be the one to give spiritual advices to the people and public. He will, at the same time, fulfil all the needy things to his wife and children. He will be satisfied in this life and he will be a very happy person.

6. He will enjoy his life and, at the same time, also enjoy all the luxury in this world but not get attached to it. By following the advice of Brahma Maharishi, for sure he will lead a genuine life in a good way with all such good things in this present life. By having this reading, it is in itself a proof of the blessings he is having from Brahma Maharishi; it is a confirmation beyond doubt that he will lead a good life.

7. Brahma Maharishi says it is indicated that he will lead his life even after the age of his 82nd running year also. With this, the 1st General chapter is concluded by Maharishi blessings.

SUBHAM.

Santhi Kandam
13th CHAPTER

This child was, in his previous incarnation, born in Sera Desam as a male child. He was born near to a hill and seashore region. (Sera Desam is now known as a region between Goa and Karnataka in India).

2. Being a male child he lived in this hilly related region. He was living with some good knowledge and developed himself on a good level. But he involved himself with some bad friendships. Because of these friendships, he was also involved in some bad events.

3. He was an unmarried man and he did not always treat the opposite sex in a good way. He disliked very much spirituality. As this continued, he disturbed the sadhus while they were doing meditation. By facing this disturbance the sadhus had a lot of difficulties and didn't have the spiritual satisfaction and peace while doing meditation. He caused them quite a lot of problems; because of this they didn't even have a permanent and quiet place to do their meditation. So, they were mentally disturbed.

4. Besides that he led his life without much worry or concern in a happy manner. But during his old age, and in the first part of his present life, he would have to suffer from a lot of obstacles to his life and it was difficult to lead his life in a peaceful manner day by day. He had to go through marital problems and separation from some close people. He roamed around here and there and it was not easy to obtain peace of mind and find the proper and happy place to settle permanently. This and more so alike is all because of the disturbances to the sadhus and his mental outlook overall in his previous birth.

5. By this incident only he is facing many more obstacles and bad events in this life. However, during his old age, he came to realize his mistakes and bad behavior. By realizing his spiritual mistakes, he started to help some orphan children, old age orphans, poor people, mentally affected persons, disabled children, blind peoples, etc. And, especially, he tried to help the spiritual persons. But whenever he tried he had to confront much opposition and sometimes he was unable to do it. He tried a lot to do service to the temples also. But also this was not always successful.

6. Up to the last period of his life he was unable to fulfil the spiritual service and helping others as otherwise wished for. By this he suffered a lot and later on he met death. By understanding his mistakes and efforts he got this birth as a human being. Maharishi is advising and blessing him to minimize his past karmic effect and then for sure he has to lead a good life with his wife and children in this present incarnation.

7. Maharishi is blessing him to overcome whatever may come and that he will have a good and a successful life. Maharishi's blessings are also there for a very long life so that he will lead his life even after the age of 82nd year running. With this, Mr. Craig's previous life chapter is concluded by Brahma Maharishi, saying that he will have one more birth as an elevated soul and finally liberated in his next birth.

SUBHAM

14th CHAPTER – DEKSHA KANDAM PANCHATCHARAM MOOLA MANTHRA "NAMASIVAYA"

This candidate is suggested to chant or listen to this "Namasivaya" Mantra for 3 Mandalas. One Mandala is 48 days, so 3x48=144 days. He should chant or listen to this Mantra two times a day. In the morning before 6 am. After his bath and in the evening after 6 pm. Each time 508 times. This will help him to overcome all obstacles and pave the way for a deep peace within.

Note: It is not the exact number of recitation of a mantra that is important. More important is it that one is reciting this Maha mantra by heart without a doubt or thought. If so performed, miracles will happen continuously.

SUBHAM

Ghana Kandam
Brahma Sukshma Naadi

Brahma Maharishi is speaking directly to him, saying that he is only got this and some few other opportunities to have these predictions after meeting many obstacles in his life but now the time has come in accordance with his karma and punyam.

Listen to me dear son; in your 65th year running you will meet and experience many spiritual events and you will involve and plunge deeper and deeper into spirituality. Eliminating gradually, all that is not relevant to enjoy true bliss and peace of mind.

Between your 62nd – 64th year running, you will get some major spiritual contacts and opportunities in your life.

But you will also have to meet some obstacles such as mental confusions, cheatings, unwanted travels on your path etc. Especially you will face some difficulties regarding spirituality or not able to seeing things crystal clear. Therefore free yourself from all concepts and ideas of what is right and wrong. Let go of fear and desires for this and that externally and internally as well. You and all others are already perfect beings and wherever you look or people you may meet, if their message is this as said here, then it will do you all the good to listen to such words. Or even better he who speaks the language of silence, him you should cherish as your own true and most happy self, for he is no other than your true liberated self.

To minimize the obstacles and to come clear of some illusions and concepts, you are advised to fulfil the spiritual suggestions of Brahma Maharishi.

And after performing these spiritual advices and by minimizing your past karma, you will get a good spiritual advisor and guide. This spiritual advisor will lead you into a good spiritual path.

You will be supported and good care will be taken by your family members. You will travel to India on a spiritual pilgrimage/visit/journey. And there you will learn many spiritual matters of great importance and all that will make a great impact on all future events thereafter in your life.

It will be so deep and useful on your spiritual path. You will develop so much power and knowledge, enabling you to do exceptional high spiritual advice, consultancy, teaching and so on at a much higher level than ever before.

You will become a saint like being. Wishing only to do good and helping others to obtain peace of mind. In this process also, you will get good spiritual assistants in your life. These spiritual assistants will be both male and female. You will then also possess great opportunities to set up an Ashram-like institution in your country.

You will do more and more spiritual service. Your birth aim is to do spiritual service to the people. Many people will come to utilize your spiritual service. You will write some spiritual books. Through these books also many people will be helped and benefitted.

Up to your last breath you will have the growing fame and name and get a high responsibility on behalf of spirituality.

Up to the last breath also you will continuously get the right help and guidance from spiritual experts. If you follow and do the spiritual advice of Maharishi, you can minimize your past karmic effect and by this, you will be able to fulfil yourself spiritually in your life.

You will achieve a lot within and in regards to helping the world as such through spirituality. You will do many good deeds and be able to help people come out of the darkness/illusions through spirituality.

You will have a next birth. That birth will be your last and completely liberated and spiritual birth. You will be happy as an innocent child and you will be able to heal all the sorrows of those coming to you. All this is possible for you and the punya and blessings are there for all this to come true. So much said and after following the advices of the Maharishis, then beyond doubt you will fulfil your life and come to live as a very happy being. He will hereafter have all the good life developments in life. What else is there to say other than he is having our blessings. With this Braham Maharishi ends this Gnana Kandam.

SUBHAM

SUGGESTED PUJA

1. Leaf / Guru donation as per his wish.
2. Puja materials as per his wish.
3. Complete clothes donation to 2 Sadhus.
4. Food donation to Sadhus in Maharishi's Ashram equal to his age.
5. He is advised to visit and the blessings in Maharishi's Ashram.
6. A milk Abishekam to Lord Shiva.
7. An Archana and Abishekam to Lord Ganapathi.
8. Cow and calf donation to a poor female.
9. A Puja performance to Goddess Parvathi.
10. If he wish our people to perform any of the above then there may be some travel expense involved.
11. Also if he wish for us to help him having the Moola Mantra Puja performed for the 3 mandalas, there will be some expenses involved. But the best way to perform any remedy is to do it by oneself and with the heart in full bhakti.
12. Best if he himself undertakes a pilgrimage to certain spiritual spots and holy places. He himself will know where to go.

With this, this Brahma Sukshma Naadi ends with Maharishis blessings.

SUBHAM

Other Kandams
2nd to 12th & 16th Chapters

BRAHMA SUKSHMA NAADI

2ND KANDAM

This Kandam informs about family, wealth, education, eyesight, speech and face.

Brahma Maharishis says:

During this period he will have the sufficient income. Delayed income and related issues will be minimized. Income related obstacles will be minimized. He will get more income through spiritual related business such as advice, teaching etc. This he will do in accordance with a special guide and abroad related eminent spiritual being, whom he already have been informed about but also other spiritual people will he connect more and more to. If he feels for it, he may also be helpful to those with special problems and ways to minimize the past karmic effects and to guide them to lead a good life without facing too much of problems and obstacles. Spiritual services to other people will help him lead a good and fulfilled life and help him to overcome whatever may come his way. There will be sufficient income to his family.

He will have some eye related health issues. This will be minimized through spiritual proceedings, spiritual exercises and also through innovative treatments. During this and in the coming period he will change his food preferences and take more and more vegetarian foods with full enjoyment.

He will possess a peaceful life within his family. He will possess a good chance to lead a good life with his wife, children and grandchildren. Also he will possess a good mutual relationship with his siblings. His family members will encourage him a lot to do the spiritual related service. His children won't have separation in their life. They will possess a good chance to live together. He won't possess any such or further problems with the first wife.

He will have a thick relationship with the second wife with the blessings of Maharishi. His family members will be more benefitted on behalf of him and his spiritual service to others.

He will enjoy and make use of the world through some technological items. He will do spiritual service to the people by using the science, computer and technology. He will be more interested to know more about new things and spiritual events/knowledge. By gathering together innovative things about spirituality, he will write more articles, journals and books with the blessings of Maharishi. Publication of books will be done without any obstacles. Through this many countrymen and others will be benefitted. They will praise him a lot for his knowledge and ideas by reading his works. He will have a growing responsibility on behalf of the public people and spiritual related persons.

Maharishi is blessing him to lead a more and more spiritual life up to your last period of his life. He will grow more in spirituality as his age grows. Often he will possess a chance to meet spiritual Masters and Siddhars. He will possess a chance to meet such highly evolved beings in Darshan, visions or alive and he will possess a chance to visit their places. He will possess worldwide spiritual communication abilities. People will love his speech and advices more. He will attain a high level of spirituality so, in due time, also to give spiritual blessings to some people coming to see him.

As a birth aim, it will good to him if he helps others in ways he has knowledge about and it can well be part of his destiny to suggest others also how to possible minimize past karmic effects through his spiritual guidance and at the same time he will seek to lead them to live a good life in a good way. By doing this the people will grow high with his own growth. In future he will possess a chance to get the spiritual blessings of Rishis and Siddhas.

- SUBHAM

Note from Kim: From here on we have done little or no transcribing, commenting)

3RD KANDAM

This Kandam gives details about the seeker's siblings. It provides details about the positive and negative aspects of the sibling's relationship.

During this period he will possess a good relationship with his brother and sister. They will admire you to lead a good life. You will advise more and you will help them. They will lead their life separately. You will possess misunderstanding with your siblings. But it will be minimized as soon as possible. There will be some miserable incidents in your sister's life. This is because of your sister's past karmic effect. Your sister will lead a good life with your guidance by minimizing her karmic effect. Your siblings may possess a chance to meet some obstacles in their life. You will get good things and good praising from your siblings. On behalf of them you will lead a good life. If you possess any obstacle on behalf of your siblings, it will be minimized with the blessings of Maharishi.
- SUBHAM

4TH KANDAM
(This chapter gives the details about the candidate's Mother, House, Vehicles, Land, Etc.,)

His mother will have some health problems. Through this she will have some medical expense. This candidate will suffer a lot. He will love his mother a lot. His mother may possess a chance to meet some obstacle. Especially she may meet some miserable condition. And also Maharishi said her spiritual advice. This miserable situation will be minimized by God's grace and by medical treatment. An AYUSH HOMAM is advised by Maharishi to minimize her obstacle. His mother will advise and support him a lot. He will possess a chance to purchase his own house. He will possess a chance to build a new house. He will possess a good chance to purchase a luxurious car. He will have some investments. He will purchase lands in high level but in low cost. He will be a popular figure in spirituality whereas worldwide peoples will appreciate and will praise him a lot through spirituality. Peoples will lead a genuine with your spiritual guidance. You will get more communication with the spiritual figures. He will face some good situations in his family. Also he will lead a happy family. He will gain more respect on behalf of their children up to the last period. You will lead a happy family life only with the spiritual service.
- Subam

5TH KANDAM

(This chapter gives the details about the candidate's Children Birth, Life span, Achievements, Problems, Death Etc. It also suggests remedial measures for the sake of the candidate's children life.)

During this period he will honored on behalf of his children. His children will keep more affection on him. His children will live together without any conflict. They will possess some misunderstanding, but it will be minimized as soon as possible. His children will get a good job or business in good level. They will earn more income to lead their life in good level. His children will be more talented with the blessings of Maharishi. His children will have a good marriage life (But with some obstacles) and also they will get children according to their well and wish. His grandchildren will possess a chance to study the higher education in good level. Her children marriage life will be good. They will have good marriage after meeting some obstacle in their life. Some unwanted problems will happen to his children. His children may have the separation in their family life. In some instance there will be a dissatisfied marriage life. This candidate has to take more care on his children family life because they are having "THARA DOSHA". This will be minimized with the blessings of Maharishi. To minimize this she has to do an Abhisheka and Archana to Goddess Parvathi on one Friday. Maharishi advised her Children to do the MANGALYA DOSHA as a remedy to minimize the family life negative events. Mangalya Dosha is nothing but she has to donate a 9 Grams (9 Kazhanjiyam) GOLD THALI to Goddess Parvathi. This will be worn in the Goddess neck. It will be forever in the Goddess neck. At last it will be safeguarded by the temple trust. His daughter's husband will do the needy things to this candidate up to the last period of the life span as equal to a Male child. After performing Maharishi's advice there won't be any such separation in the marriage life to her children. Her children health will be good. Her children will have a mutual understanding with her husband. Her children marriage life will be good. Her children won't have any such separation, if she follows the spiritual advice of Maharishi. He and his children will possess a thick relationship up to the last period.

- Subam

Mr. Craig – Chapter 6
(This chapter gives the details about diseases, their causes and damages, etc. It provides the information about enemies, litigation etc. It also suggests remedial measures for the negative events. It guides to achieve success in the life.)

He will possess breathing problem, indigestion problem etc. He has to intake natural foods and vegetarian foods. As this continuation he has to follow the spiritual exercises such as Yoga, Meditation etc. Maharishi is advising that this candidate will have opposite persons in the business field. But those opposite persons will come and surrender with this candidate in the day to day life. No one can win this candidate by opposing him. He will meet some conflicts and problems by the opposite persons. Meanwhile this candidate will get victory. He won't have loan problem up to the last period. He will face some obstacles in the economic status. Through this he will face the income related issues. But he won't get loans and he won't struggle to repay the loans etc. He will face some property related court case. But at last he will get success in the court case.

- Subam

Mr. Craig – Chapter 7
(This chapter gives the details about the Marriage related details. Remedial measures to minimize the negative events in the marriage life.)

In this generation you will possess a chance to have two wives. But you will live with only one wife permanently up to the last period. This wife support will be an added advantage to your life development. She will guide you and support you a lot. You might face some marriage related issues in this generation. This is happened because of the past karmic effect. The present life will be good to you. You will lead a genuine life in this generation. You and your wife will possess a thick relationship. Your family life will be good. You can achieve a good life development with your wife support. She will take responsibility of your administration. You won't face separation with the misunderstanding, conflict etc. with the present wife. Your wife will do service to you up to her last period.

- Subam

8TH KANDAM

(This chapter gives the information about the candidate's Life span, Accidents, Obstacles occurring.)

In this generation your birth is a blessed one. Your birth is a precious one for the peoples around the world. You have the destiny to minimize the past karmic effect to the worldwide peoples and to show them a good way and guide them; to lead a good life in this generation is your destiny. You will attain the popularity and publicity in a short period with the blessings of Maharishi. You will declare as a role model to the peoples in spirituality. Peoples will be jealous on you and your life because of your spiritual development. You must be aware of vehicles. There may be vehicle accidents as advised by Maharishi. In this generation there will be some obstacles in your life as advised by Maharishi. Maharishi advises you to be aware in your life. You may meet some natural obstacles and accidents in your life. You can minimize all the negative effects if you follow the advice of Maharishi in good level.

As per Maharishi, then this seeker will merge with God at the age of his 82nd year running. He will merge with God in the early morning during the snow/winter season particularly in the sleeping time between 3am to 5am in the morning.

SUBHAM

9TH KANDAM

(This chapter gives the details about the candidate's Ancestral property, about his father, Wealth, Spiritual inclinations, Spiritual worshipping and Guruji's blessings etc.)

In this generation you possessed a chance to get this prediction from Maharishi after your father's death. This is your destiny blessed by Maharishi. But all your efforts in your life will get success with the blessings of Maharishi. You will have more spiritual involvement while getting this prediction. You will face more development in your life after getting the advice from Maharishi. During this period you will go to abroad country to the spiritual purpose. You might possess a chance to get your Guruji's blessings. Meeting the Rishis and Siddhis is provided to you in this life. After getting the blessings you

will possess a chance to do the spiritual service to the worldwide peoples with the abroad related spiritualist. This spiritual service includes giving spiritual advice and teaching to the peoples. You will guide the peoples to minimize their karmic effect, to lead their life in good level. You will do help to the Orphans, Old age peoples and mentally retarded peoples, etc. You will possess a chance to spread spirituality to the peoples through the mode of Light and Sound. You are blessed person of Maharishi. Often you will attain the blessings of God through Rishis by going to the abroad country as advised by Maharishi. This is nothing, but you will go to abroad country often to receive the blessings of Maharishi.
- Subam

Mr. Craig – Chapter 10
(This chapter gives the details about the candidate's Business life. Profits and losses in the business. Remedy to rectify the business, etc.)

Maharishi is blessing that you will have a new business. This business is related to abroad country related spiritual service. You will declare as a spiritual guide to the worldwide peoples. Maharishi is telling that in your 63rd age you will face a good spiritual development. Your spiritual advice to the peoples will be true to them and also more effective to the peoples. Your spiritual advice to the peoples will be realized. You will face a good achievement in spirituality with the blessings of Maharishi. Peoples will observe you as a role model in spirituality. You will lead a peaceful life. There will be a peaceful life to you hereafter than before. You will meet both God and Maharishi through dream. You will get a good responsibility by the spiritualists wherever you go. All the obstacles activities will get success to you and your business. You or your family members will possess a chance to go to the abroad visit for the spiritual visit. You will get a good spiritual guidance from the abroad country spiritual people. Their guidance will give you a good development in your spiritual life. You will possess a chance to get spiritual assistants and spiritual followers in this generation. You will get sufficient income without any obstacles. There will be a good understanding with your family members. You will make a good achievement in spirituality. Especially Maharishi is blessing in astrological services and by minimizing the past karmic effect to the people to lead a good and peaceful life. You will have a good healthy life. If you have some physical issues, it will be minimized. You will observe more spiritual events day by day. You will grow more in spirituality. You will write the spiritual books regularly without any obstacle. Peoples will purchase this in high level to know more about spiritual events. Maharishi is blessing that you will be an eminent person in media field. You will get a chance to know more about the new technologies about media. There will be some health issues such as indigestion and bone related issues. But this will be minimized through treatments and with the blessings of Maharishi. Maharishi is advising to follow the spiritual exercises. You will get the blessings of siddhis through dream. And also there is a chance to make conversations with them through dream. You will possess a chance to write books about the research of Rishis and siddhis. You will spread an Ashram. You will get income through various aspects. You will get assistants in your administration. You will like to lead a simple life in general. You will fulfil the needy things of your family members in good level. The peoples who were benefitted will pray you and praise you a lot. Continuously you will follow the meditational practices. During this period you will possess a chance to spread an Ashram in the abroad country with the guidance of the spiritual peoples. This Ashram may be spread in your own place in the abroad country. All your assets will change as immovable properties. You will register this as a Trust. You will possess a chance to lead a good and peaceful life by minimizing your past karmic effect. You will do business and service related to spirituality and media. All your spiritual thoughts will be fulfilled by the worldwide peoples. –Subam

11TH KANDAM

(This chapter gives the details about the candidate's Conveyance and Second Marriage. Remedy to rectify the Negatives.)

You will get a good income through spirituality. You will get more income through astrological service and by minimizing the past karmic effect to the worldwide peoples. Media field will support you a lot to get more income. You will get more income and you will meet unexpected good development within 63rd age to 68th age. You will possess a chance to get honor awards and cash awards by the government. You will get the fulfilment of your children. Your children will fulfil your needy things up to the last period of your life. Your children will take more care on you, your wife and also in the business. Your children will guide you without hesitation. The present wife will be with you up to your life end. She will do service to you till the life end. Your wife support will give you more development in your spiritual service and business through administration. You will get income through consultancy field. You will get more benefits through the present wife. You won't have income related issues. You will have deposits. SUBHAM

Mr. Craig – Chapter 12

(This chapter gives the information about your expenditure of money. About the way of spending the money, the way in which it happened; it also explains about Moksha or heavenly status, any monetary benefits, higher status arising from foreign tours and foreign contacts. It also deals with your next birth that is where you will be born, what will be your living conditions, etc. Remedial advice to minimize the negatives.)

Maharishi is blessing that you will get continuous income and this income will change as deposits to your life. Maharishi is telling that you may have unwanted expense also. Maharishi is advising that you have to change this unwanted expense into good things such as spreading ashram in abroad country, doing spiritual expense in abroad country, doing expense to the children's spirituality, buying house etc. You will be more eager to know more about spiritual places. You often will go to visit the places of Rishis's living place and to get blessings from them. You will possess a chance to make interview the rishis and siddhis to write books. Often you will travel to abroad country for the above said events. Moksha is not advised to you in this generation as advised by Maharishi. You have your next birth as a human being in the abroad country. This birth is advised in the spiritual place where siddhis are living and lived. Especially your birth is advised in the Sozha desam. You birth is advised a male. You will start your spiritual service in your young stage. You will be a familiar person in your young stage through spiritual services. You will get the full blessings of God and Maharishi. Remedy: You have to contribute some spiritual donation to the temple in your previous birthplace. This donation can be given as your well and wish to the temple. This donation is to be utilized to the repairing works, additional constructional works, painting works etc. The above said remedy is said to get the blessings of Maharishi and to make achievements in the above said events (in the 12th chapter reading). – Subam

15TH KANDAM will follow soon.

Mr. Craig – Chapter 16
(This chapter gives the information about the social service and political life.)

Maharishi is advising that at present Saturn period (Disa) is in process. In that Venus bhukthi is in process.

At present the period is nice and also a lucky period to this gentleman.

During this period this candidate will possess a chance to more spiritual involvement. He will possess chances to meet many more spiritual places and also to the abroad country visit. Through this he will be more happy, peaceful and satisfied. In his family he will possess a good understanding with his family members. He will possess a chance to have good functions and events in his family. His wife, family members, siblings will keep more affection on him a lot. They will guide him and obey him a lot. He will have more spiritual involvement in high level. He will do the business and service related to spirituality. This indicates advice, teaching, astrological field, etc. He will do the spiritual events such as to minimize the past karmic effect to lead their life in good level. His spiritual service will play a vital role to the worldwide people. He will have a stable life with a good health as blessed by Maharishi. His health issues will be in his control. He will possess a good flow in income. He will purchase assets in good level such as house, land, vehicle etc. He will have assistants always in his life. His assistants will fulfil his needy things. He will face unexpected good events in his life in common and also through spirituality. He will get government related help and guidance. He will be praised by the public peoples. All your thoughts will get success during 63rd to 68th age. He will reach and spread the spirituality through innovative technologies. Peoples will inhale a lot. Also he will get a good feedback. Particularly he will declare as spiritual guide to the peoples to solve the problem of peoples. He will show a good way to the worldwide peoples. His assistants will guide him and will help him a lot. He will get a spiritual related business in this period especially. This will be blessed up to his last life. You will get a good response on behalf of the public peoples at any time. His children and grandchildren will keep more affection and also they will take more care about him. His sibling's children also will keep more affection and also they will obey him a lot. But they will lead their family separately. The next half of the life is blessed with spirituality by Maharishi to him. He will do spiritual related service and business. Through this he will lead a good peaceful life with spiritual blessings. After getting this advice he will have a powerful life. He will be respected by the public peoples. Maharishi prescribed some puja advises to him in general. All the spiritual words, advice and blessings of Maharishi will be true to him and it will give more effects in his life if he follows his spiritual advice.

SUBHAM

Tips about Finding a Naadi Reader

I do not offer a Naadi reading service or give out the names and addresses of credible readers. I have already been overwhelmed with requests since my first book *Messages from the Universe* and, as I have already explained, the whole Naadi industry is so riddled with corruption that I would be horrified if I accidentally pointed someone to a charlatan. At the moment I am only introducing family and friends and a handful of people who, I believe, are on a spiritual quest, or helping me closely with my work for the Hamilton Parker Foundation. As I have also mentioned before, some Naadi readers I have used are now charging too much so I could not recommend them and, if money becomes too much a factor, then a previously good Naadi can become corrupted and the leaves themselves will not reveal the truth.

Tricks of the Trade

There are many tricks used by some unscrupulous readers to dupe 'rich' westerners and relieve them of their cash. Some use fake leaves and fill in the reading using astrology or duplicate text from other people's readings. Indian astrology can be very insightful so this may give you lots of correct information but astrology by itself is not Naadi. A complete fake will ask leading questions and may even have someone listening in the waiting room to report overheard conversations. The reader may use cold reading techniques to imply that the reader knows much more about you than he actually does. This can include giving general information until something is accepted and then elaborating on the hits to make it appear correct; using statements that seem personal but will apply to many people; telling you information that they have already had confirmed earlier in the reading; using flattery and so on. Many fraudulent psychics use the same methods, either deliberately or unconsciously.

The unscrupulous Naadi reader may add extra accidents and traumatic events to frighten you into spending extravagant amounts on the remedies. The charges for the remedies can be exaggerated and extra charges added so that the bill runs into thousands of pounds/dollars.

There are readers who use genuine leaves but, in order to 'help', either elaborate with their own interpretations using astrology or miss out critical information that may upset you – such as the predicted time of your death. Changes of emphasis and the addition of the astrologer's own interpretations may confuse things and distract from what was said by the Rishi authors. This is not a deliberate fraud, of course, but massaging the truth of what is said in the leaves may stop you knowing your destiny and remedying negative karma. Remember that Naadi readers are not clairvoyants. Most are people with no special powers who have learnt to read what is written on the leaves in ancient Tamil and have it translated it into your language. A special few have good spiritual intent, an extensive understanding of Indian philosophy and may be truly devout and spiritually minded but these, too, are fallible if they mess with what's said on the leaves. In my own consultations I have always had the leaves read exactly as written without any additional astrological information added unless I have specifically asked for this.

Since writing my books I have now met lots of readers, and some have become friends, but I have also seen hitherto wonderful readers become corrupted when exposed to the financial opportunities presented by Westerners paying too much. All of the above is, of course, great fodder for the skeptics who discount the lot and see the Naadis as schemes designed to hasten the divorce between a gullible fool and his money.

Negative Influences

The Naadi leaves are like a living thing and are very sensitive to the intent of the person who reads them as well as the person making the consultation. If your reason for consulting the leaves is coloured by greed, lust, ambition and so on then this may also affect the reading.

In the right hands, and if everything is in order, the Naadis can be 100% accurate in their predictions but sometimes a hitherto good reader may lose their accuracy – something may start to influence their readings – a materialistic motive of some kind, the shadow of Kali Yuga or the influence of the planets on the present moment. If a reader's prices suddenly go up I step away as the oracle is now contaminated and useless.

There are stories of how the leaves have told a reader to stop and give the leaves, and with them his livelihood, to someone else; a sincere reader will do as he is told and may never read the leaves again. If the leaves are used with this sort of sincerity and devotion they will tell you incredible things and take you towards self-realization. They can help with worldly issues, medical cures and will tell you all sorts of things that will help your earthly and spiritual advancement.

Finding a Genuine Reader

To find your leaves you will need to undertake a search and, if you have enough good karma, then you will eventually find what you seek. Seeking your leaf is part of the spiritual process. If it is destined, your soul will have a strong urge to seek a remedy through a Naadi leaf reading.

You can start your research on the Internet though I have found that some readers charge from $200 to $1,000 US to access the kandams (chapters) or the Prasana kandam, which will answer 5 specific questions after the main chapter has been opened. This does not include any remedies, which can run into many more thousands if you are not careful. I was quoted $1,000 to ask five questions of the Prasana Kandam on the Internet, from an excellent reader I had used before, but with other contacts I was able to ask the same 5 questions of the Bhrugu Samhita for $162 – quite a mark-up! This susceptibility of the readers to contamination is the reason I cannot simply recommend readers to people who ask.

My first Naadi readings were free, as my friends organized them for me. Later we paid about $85 US per chapter for myself and for other people whom I introduced to the services. The cost of remedies will vary depending on what's needed. These can cost from $400 to $1,000 US. As you can see, it can all become quite expensive if you select the wrong reader and you will see why this is all subject to so much corruption as these figures are enormous amounts to earn compared with average earnings of Indian villagers.

You can find a list of addresses for the Naadi Shastris Centres in the book 'Naadi Predictions' by Wing Commander Shashikant Oak. This is available on Amazon and is an excellent book with lots of fascinating examples from people who have had readings. Kim Paisol's books *Naadi Palmleaf Astrology* and his new book *Compassion: Bhagavan Sri Ramana, Naadis, Pothis and Samhitas* are also fascinating books, with lots of guidance and information, and are both available from Amazon.

When you find a reader, don't expect to enjoy an efficient, seamless service. Many of the readers are from easy-going rural India and are not particularly punctual or organized. For example I was let down three times when I sat for my first Skype consultation but it was worth the wait. It is also possible that your leaves may not be there in the set that the reader has, as many were destroyed at the time of the British Raj.

Safeguarding Yourself

I wanted to test the oracle when I wrote my first book so I did a number of readings with unconnected readers so that I could compare the information given about me and the predictions for my future. Initially I had two separate readings with two readers, introduced to me by my friend Vivek. These were the Naadi readers I spoke about in my book *Messages from the Universe*. This gave me a way to verify what was being said from two separate sources.

Later I accessed the readings described in this book with people introduced to me by Kim Paisol. I paid the readers directly for the reading and visited the Naadi reader in India to do the remedies. I paid him directly, partly by money transfer and, afterwards in India, by cash. My case will be different from yours as I was in the luxurious position of having been introduced by trustworthy people who monitored and supervised my progress. I now do the same for friends and family who want to consult the Naadis.

When you book or start your reading, do not give away information about yourself. There are services on the Internet, which tell you to fill out questionnaire forms that ask for your thumbprint, plus the names of all your family, the time and place of your birth, how many brothers and sisters you have, if you are married and have children, if you have health problems, legal problems and so on. Now, it may be that this request is quite innocent as, with it, they can find your leaf, but to us, skeptical westerners, this is clearly not good practice.

It is best to give as little information as possible and use email addresses and Skype accounts that reveal nothing about who you are. Not only will this ensure that no cheating occurs but it will also help convince you of the reality of the Naadi and the changes you will later make to your destiny. The depth of your sincerity will influence the remedies so it's important not to harbour doubts because you were not thorough at the start.

If they have your thumbprint they can find your bundle and you will be asked a series of questions until the appropriate leaf is found. You will be able to tell, from the type of questions asked in the leaf finding process, if the reader is true. I have already described in this book and *Messages from the Universe* how this process works. Download the appropriate software, test it in advance, and record everything on Skype or tape so you can go over it all later. This should apply to both the leaf finding session and the predictions session.

Doing your Remedies

By now you will have a good idea about what the remedies are and why we need to do them. You can try to do them yourself or have someone do them for you – preferably someone you are related to by blood or, alternatively, by the Naadi reader or a Hindu priest. Some people do not do the remedies at all and let fate take its course. I advise you to do them soon after the reading if you can afford it or do them at some point later in your life. I have heard of cases where the remedies were too much for the person to afford but, as soon as they made a start doing them for themselves, their circumstances radically changed and the money was suddenly there to have the rest completed.

The complexity of the remedies will vary from person to person. They can sometimes cost a lot – my remedies included buying a woman a cow, feeding a school of children, helping beggars and extensive rituals across India. There will also be included your personal mantras to chant that can take hundreds of hours or can be done by proxy. I paid the reader directly, as I was confident of their authenticity, but you may decide to get a second quotation from the services I have suggested.

The oracle will foretell good and bad things in your life. All these are a result of your karma and some things may not be possible to change. However the Maharishi seers who wrote the leaves also include spiritual 'remedies' that you can do to reduce or remove the negative effects of karma carried forward from past lives. It is best to do these yourself, although they can also be done by proxy – that is, one of the Naadi readers can do the mantras, human, temple visits or get a priest to do them for you. There may also be charitable acts to be done that you can do yourself or pay to have done. As I say, if possible do these yourself as some Naadi readers skimp or simply do not deliver these services for you.

It is important also to get evidence that your remedies have been done. When I have ordered remedies by proxy for myself, or others, the Naadi reader will be sent a photograph of whom the remedies are for. For example, I had a remedy to be done for my mother's health so I sent a picture of her that was then held by the people doing the remedies. If a beggar was being fed, or an Ayusha Homam being performed, the photo would be included in the scenes that were put onto video and posted to me afterwards. Having everything on video confirms that the remedies have been done and done properly and, by watching the videos, we also become more engaged with what's happening and add our spirit to the proceedings. If possible it's best to go to India and participate directly but this may not be possible for everyone. I went to India to do the most important remedies and paid for a few rituals – such as the mantra chanting – to be done by priests in India.

It is not always necessary to have the Naadi reader do the remedies or buy them for you. There are services in India – and now on the Internet – that can have any of the rituals and remedies done for you. Get some quotations and compare prices. If the Naadi reader's prices are fair and you trust him then you can use his services. If his prices are high, go elsewhere. Although we are dealing with mind-boggling mystical things that will throw you into a whirlwind of baffled wonder, it's still important to use common sense and scrutiny when paying. The Naadi may be sacred but the people interpreting it are fallible.

Did you Enjoy this Book?

If you enjoyed this book, please leave a testimonial and rating on Amazon. Your positive comments help me to reach more people and share the philosophy of spirit.

www.amazon.com
www.amazon.co.uk

Follow me on YouTube

I produce a weekly vlog for YouTube in which I talk about and address some of the philosophical implications of this book. I try, whenever time allows, to interact through the comments posts. If you have any observations and questions, please join me on YouTube.

https://www.youtube.com/user/psychicmovies

Check out our Website

You can also read much more about Jane and my work as mediums on our website:

www.psychics.co.uk

Glossary

Aarati also spelled arti, arati, arathi, aarthi is a Hindu religious ritual of worship, a part of puja, in which light from wicks soaked in ghee or camphor is offered to one or more deities. In Sanskrit, the word 'arti' – transcribed as 'aarati' – is composed of the prefix 'aa', meaning complete, and 'rati', meaning love. The arti is thus an expression of one's complete and unflinching love towards God.

Archana A special, personal, abbreviated *puja* done by temple priests in which the name, birth star, and family lineage of a devotee are recited to invoke individual guidance and blessings. *Archana* also refers to chanting the names of the deity, which is a central part of every *puja*. The Sanskrit meaning is "honoring, praising."

Astral relating to a supposed non-physical realm of existence to which various psychic and paranormal phenomena are ascribed, and in which the physical human body is said to have a counterpart.

Ayanamsa is the Sanskrit term in Indian astronomy for the amount of precession. In astrology, this is the longitudinal difference between the Tropical (Sayana) and Sidereal (Nirayana) zodiacs.

Ayusha Homam is a fire ritual that is performed for long life and removal of all obstacles. It is done to worship the god of life Ayur Devatha.

Brahman The highest Universal Principle, the Ultimate Reality in the universe. In major schools of Hindu philosophy, it is the material, efficient, formal and final cause of all that exists. Most Hindus believe that Brahman is present in every person as the eternal spirit or soul, called the atman.

Chiranjivi The seven immortal living beings who are to remain alive on Earth until the end of the current Kali Yuga.

Darshan (Sanskrit: "viewing") an opportunity to see, or an occasion of seeing a holy person or the image of a deity.

Diksha (also spelled *deeksha* or *deeksa*, translated as a "preparation or consecration for a religious ceremony"). Giving of a mantra or an initiation by the guru.

Guru dana or *daana* is the virtue of generosity or giving, a form of alms.

Kala Bhairava A fierce manifestation of Shiva associated with annihilation. He originated in Hindu mythology and is sacred to Hindus, Buddhists, and Jains alike. He is worshiped in Nepal, Rajasthan, Karnataka, Tamil Nadu, and Uttarakhand.

Kriya Yoga is a the ancient Yoga system revived in modern times by Mahavatar Babaji and brought to the West by Paramhansa Yogananda, author of Autobiography of a Yogi.

Kundalini The primal energy, or *shakti*, located at the base of the spine.

Moksha (also called *vimoksha*, *vimukti*, and *mukti*). Liberation, emancipation, Self-realization, or release.

Murugan (Kartikeya) The god whom the Tamils regard as their own. He is the same as Subrahmanya, Skanda (Kanda), Karttikeya, or Kumara. The name means "beautiful." A lot of Tamil hymnal literature is devoted to him, of which the Tiruppugazh is particularly famous. Lord Murugan was born by the divine spark from Lord Shiva, and he is very popular among Tamil-speaking people. He is worshiped for prosperity and protection from evil. He is the second son of Lord Shiva and Goddess Parvathi. He is often shown as having six faces. His chariot is driven by a peacock. He is the general for warriors of the angels in the fights against evil. He is worshiped for health and wealth.

Naadi Naadi is the collective name for the palm-leaf manuscripts, dictated by ancient sages, predicting the characteristics, family history, as well as the careers of people who will consult the oracle. Scholars in different parts of India have in their safekeeping several **granthas** (volumes) of the palm-leaf manuscripts. Naadi is an ancient astrology, which has been composed by great *maharishis* of ancient India, using their precognitive spiritual powers. The volumes were dictated by the great sages, including Bhrugu, Vasistha, Agastya, Shukra, and others. The sages recorded predictions for every individual for the betterment of humanity and to safeguard *dharma* (righteousness). There are two types of Naadi—Maha Sukshma are written as one long dialogue between Shiva and his consort Parvathi; the others are divided into chapters.

Naadi Grantham Nadi astrology is generally referred to as Nadi Grantham in South India and Bhrighu Samitham in the North. (Naadi is sometimes spelt with a single 'a'.)

Naadi Shastra Naadi Science.

Pancha Bhoota Stalam refers to the five Shiva temples dedicated to

Shiva, each representing the manifestation of the five prime elements of nature: land, water, air, sky, fire. *Pancha* indicates Five, *Bhoota* means elements and *Stala* means place.

Panchakshara Mantra (also called the *Panchakshara stotra*). The *Panchakshara* literally means "five letters" in Sanskrit and refers to the five holy letters "Na," "Ma," "Si," "Va," and "Ya." This is a prayer to Lord Shiva, and it is associated with Shiva's mantra "Om Namah Shivaya."

Prarabdha Karma The part of sanchita karma, a collection of past karmas, which are ready to be experienced through the present body (incarnation). According to Sri Swami Sivananda: "Prarabdha is that portion of the past karma which is responsible for the present body. That portion of the sanchita karma which influences human life in the present incarnation is called prarabdha. It is ripe for reaping. It cannot be avoided or changed. It is only exhausted by being experienced. You pay your past debts. Prarabdha karma is that which has begun and is actually bearing fruit. It is selected out of the mass of the sanchita karma."

Puja (Sometimes spelt phonetically as pooja or poojah.) A religious ritual performed as an offering to various deities, distinguished persons, or special guests. Some Hindus perform *puja* every morning after bathing and dressing but prior to taking any food or drink. *Puja* is seen as a way of linking humans to the divine, and it can be performed for anything considered holy.

Prasad a devotional offering made to a god, typically consisting of food that is later shared among devotees.

Rishi A holy Hindu sage, saint, or inspired poet. *Maharishi*—great saint. *Saptarishi*—the seven patriarchs of the Vedic religion.

Sadhana (Sanskrit, "a means of accomplishing something"). An ego-transcending spiritual practice.

Sannyasa The final life-stage of renunciation within the Hindu philosophy of four, age-based life-stages known as *ashrams*, with the previous three being *brahmacharya* (bachelor student), *grihastha* (householder), and *vanaprastha* (forest dweller, retired).

Shanti (also *santhi* or *shanthi*, from Sanskrit meaning "be calm"). Peace, rest, calmness, tranquility, or bliss.

Shastra The knowledge which is based on principles that are held to be timeless. It is also a byword used when referring to a scripture such as a treatise or text written in explanation of some idea. The palm leaves are often called the *Naadi Shastra*.

Shiva (Sanskrit, "The Auspicious One"), also known as *Mahadeva* ("Great God"), is one of the main deities of Hinduism. Shiva is worshiped as the destroyer and restorer of worlds and in numerous other forms. Shiva is often conceived as a member of the *Trimurti*, along with Brahma and Vishnu.

Sapta Rishis Naadi astrologers believe that palm leaves were written by the sapta rishis or the great seven of all the rishis. These are Sage Vashista, Sage Agasthya, Sage Bhrighu, Sage Viswamitra, Sage Valmiki, Sage Bohar and Sage Vyasar. (Veda Vyasar – the famed author of Mahabharata). It is believed that these sages gave the palm leaves to seven families and their descendants are the modern-day Naadi readers.

Srimad Bhagavatam is one of Hinduism's eighteen great Puranas. (Mahapuranas, great histories.) It promotes bhakti (devotion) to Krishna.

Siddha an ascetic who has achieved enlightenment.

Swarga (or *svarga*), also known as *swarga loka*, is one of the seven *loka* or planes in Hindu cosmology, which, sequentially are *bhu loka* (*prithvi loka*, Earth), *bhuvar loka*, *swarga loka*, *mahar loka*, *jana loka*, *tapa loka*, and the highest, *satyaloka* (*brahmaloka*). It is a set of heavenly worlds located on and above Mount Meru. It is a heaven, where the righteous live in a paradise before their next incarnation. During each *pralaya*, the great dissolution, the first three realms, *bhu loka* (Earth), *bhuvar loka*, and *swarga loka*, are destroyed. Below the seven upper realms lie seven lower realms of *patala*, the underworld and netherworld.

Theertham The physical, holy-water body associated with a temple or deity.

Trataka The practice of fixed gazing at an external object to achieve single-pointed concentration, strengthening the eyes, and stimulating the *ajna* chakra (third eye).

Turiya The background that underlies and transcends the three common states of consciousness, which are waking consciousness, dreaming, and dreamless sleep.

Yajna literally means "sacrifice, devotion, worship, offering", and refers in Hinduism to any ritual done in front of a sacred fire, often with mantras.

Mantras

Nishprapanchaya

Nishprapanchaya is a description of one of the aspects of God—bliss—in the sequence "being-consciousness-bliss" in Hindu monotheism. As such, it is sung daily in some Hindu temples and ashrams.

Om Namah Shivaya Gurave
(Om. Salutations to the guru, who is Shiva.)
Satchidananda Murtaye
(His form is being, consciousness, and bliss.)
Nishprapanchaya Shantaya
(He is transcendent, calm.)
Niralambaya Tejase
(Free from all support, and luminous.)

Gayatri Mantra

The Gayatri Mantra is a highly revered mantra from the Vedas. Like all Vedic mantras, the Gayatri mantra is considered not to have an author and, like all other Vedic mantras, is believed to have been revealed to a brahmarshi, in this case Vishvamitra.

Oṃ bhur bhuvaḥ svaḥ

tat savitur vareṇyaṃ
bhargo devasya dhimahi
dhiyo yo naḥ pracodayat

We contemplate the glory of Light illuminating the three worlds: gross, subtle, and causal.
I am that vivifying power, love, radiant illumination, and divine grace of universal intelligence.
We pray for the divine light to illumine our minds.

Books by Craig Hamilton-Parker

Hamilton-Parker, Craig & Jane (1995) *The Psychic Workbook* Random House ISBN 0-09-179086-7 (Languages: English, Chinese)

Hamilton-Parker, Craig (1996) *Your Psychic Powers* Hodder & Stoughton ISBN 0-340-67417-2 (Languages: English)

Hamilton-Parker, Craig (1999) *Timeless Wisdom of the Tibetans* Hodder & Stoughton ISBN 0-340-70483-7 (Languages: English)

Hamilton-Parker, Craig (1999) *The Psychic Casebook* Blandford/Sterling ISBN 0-7137-2755-1 (Languages: English, Turkish)

Hamilton-Parker, Craig (1999) *The Hidden Meaning of Dreams* Sterling imprint Barnes & Noble ISBN 0-8069-7773-6 (Languages: English, Spanish, Portuguese, Russian, Israeli, Greek Icelandic.)

Hamilton-Parker, Craig (2000) *The Intuition Pack* Godfield Books ISBN 1-84181-007-X

Hamilton-Parker, Craig (2000) *Remembering Your Dreams* Sterling imprint Barnes & Noble ISBN 0-8069-4343-2

Hamilton-Parker, Craig (2000) *Unlock Your Secret Dreams* Sterling imprint Barnes & Noble ISBN 1-4027-0316-3

Hamilton-Parker, Craig (2002) *Fantasy Dreaming* Sterling imprint Barnes & Noble ISBN 0-8069-5478-7

Hamilton-Parker, Craig (2003) *Protecting the Soul* Sterling imprint Barnes & Noble ISBN 0-8069-8719-7

Hamilton-Parker, Craig (2004) *Psychic Dreaming* Sterling imprint Barnes & Noble ISBN 1-4027-0474-7

Hamilton-Parker, Craig (2005) *Opening to the Other Side* Sterling imprint Barnes & Noble ISBN 1-4027-1346-0

Hamilton-Parker, Craig (2010) *What To Do When You Are Dead* Sterling imprint Barnes & Noble ISBN 978-1-4027-7660-1 (Languages: English, Dutch, Portuguese) Published on Amazon & Kindle

Hamilton-Parker, Craig (2015) *Messages from the Universe* Amazon.com ISBN 978-1517568887

Hamilton-Parker, Craig (2000) *Intuitive Knowledge* Amazon.com ISBN 978-1535268783

Hamilton-Parker, Craig with Kipling, Violet (2014) *Psychics & Mediums Network Training Manuals* Amazon.com ISBN 1503126048

Hamilton-Parker, Craig (2014) *The Dream Handbook* Amazon.com ISBN 1503004309

Hamilton-Parker, Craig (2014) *Psychic Protection* Amazon.com ISBN 1501005642

Hamilton-Parker, Craig (2014) *A Medium's Guide to Psychic Dream Interpretation* Amazon.com ISBN 1500924474

Hamilton-Parker, Craig (2014) *Psychic School* Amazon.com ISBN 150247798X

Hamilton-Parker, Craig (2014) *Psychic Encounters* Amazon.com ISBN 1500759228

Hamilton-Parker, Craig (2014) *Tibetan Buddhism in Daily Life* Amazon.com ISBN 1502554933

Hamilton-Parker, Craig (2014) *Your Psychic Powers* Amazon.com ISBN 1500807230

You May Also Enjoy These Books by Craig Hamilton-Parker

Available from psychics.co.uk

MESSAGES FROM THE UNIVERSE

The incredible story of Craig's encounter with the Naadi Oracle of India and how it predicts the future with 100% accuracy – including the future day of his death. Craig tells the story of his encounter with the oracle and writes about the implications of fate and destiny. The book also tells of Craig and his wife Jane's work as a mediumistic couple and how they travel the world giving readings to celebrities and meet holy people as they fulfil the startling predictions made by the oracle.

This book is the prequel to 'Mystic Journey to India' and tells the mind-boggling predictions that take Craig to India to do the magic remedies.

THE DREAM BOOK TRILOGY

Read all three books in this series. In *Lucid Dreaming and Dream Recall* you are shown how to bring your dreams to life and eventually become a lucid dreamer with the ability to wake up in a dream as it is taking place. In the *Meaning of Dreams and Fantasies* you will learn to interpret and understand your dreams and fantasies. *Mystical Dream Interpretation* explains your psychic dreams and dreams about the future.

WHAT TO DO WHEN YOU ARE DEAD

"What to Do When You Are Dead is a landmark book" – Psychic News

Is there life after death? In this book Craig draws on cross cultural beliefs and his own work to describe what life is like in the afterlife. This book will help you to overcome the fear of death and prepare you for the next-life.

Based on extensive research and direct insights the book builds a picture of what the afterlife is like and what life is like on the other side.

PSYCHIC SCHOOL: HOW TO BECOME A PSYCHIC MEDIUM

Filmed over a year in a three-part documentary for the BBC, Craig and Jane Hamilton-Parker's psychic students were taught from novices to become mediums capable of working in a theatre. This book expands on the lessons seen in the programs with additional teachings from Craig's thirty years of mediumship. It takes you step-by-step from developing basic psychic powers to becoming a professional medium.

PSYCHIC PROTECTION – SAFE MEDIUMSHIP

If you are a psychic medium or someone who is very sensitive to spiritual vibrations, you are influenced by the positive or negative energies around you. Through examples from Craig and Jane's casebooks, he explains how to combat negative influences, work safely with ghosts, poltergeists, spells and spirits and how to protect your spiritual journey.

ORDER AT: psychics.co.uk

Psychics.co.uk

CLAIRVOYANCE SERVICES

Craig & Jane Hamilton-Parker offer psychic and mediumistic readings from their website. They also have an online community where you can ask questions and share your paranormal dreams and psychic insights with likeminded people.

Visit: psychics.co.uk

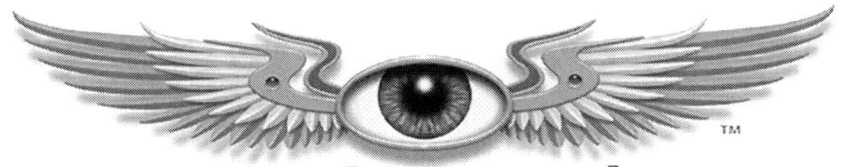

If you would like a reading today you can call their telephone psychics and book a reading on the numbers below:

UK: 0800 067 8600
USA: 1855 444 6887
EIRE: 1800 719 656
AUSTRALIA: 1800 825 305

Callers must be 18 or over to use this service and have the bill payer's permission. For entertainment purposes only. All calls are recorded. PhonePayPlus regulated SP: StreamLive Ltd, EC4R 1BB, 0800 0673 330.

The Hamilton-Parker Foundation

The Hamilton-Parker Foundation has the key objectives of spreading the teachings and messages of Craig & Jane Hamilton-Parker to the masses; establish Meditation Temples, Spiritual Education Centres, and to contribute for the causes of helping the poor, care for the environment, spiritual healing for all creatures and the safe practice of mediumship.

The Hamilton-Parker Foundation provides a family orientated haven where safe mediumship is presented in a spiritual atmosphere.

Though a worldwide network of meditation villages, trainees are invited to raise their consciousness through the powers of **concentration, meditation** and **mediumship**. The organisation also encourages a spirit of **service** with part of its resources used to directly feed the destitute and homeless.

If you would like to help with our cause, please see the page on our website: **psychics.co.uk/foundation**

About the Author

Craig Hamilton-Parker is a British author, television personality and professional psychic medium. He is best known for his TV shows *Our Psychic Family*, *The Spirit of Diana*, *Nightmares Decoded* and *Mystic Journey to India*. On television he usually works with his wife Jane Hamilton-Parker who is also a psychic medium. Their work was showcased in a three-part documentary on the BBC called *Mediums Talking to the Dead*. They now have TV shows in the USA and spend a lot of time demonstrating mediumship around the world.

Born in Southampton UK, Craig was convinced at an early age that he was mediumistic. He became a well-known as a platform medium within Spiritualism and in 1994 left his job as advertising executive to become the resident psychic on Channel 4 television's *The Big Breakfast* making predictions for upcoming news stories. He wrote a regular psychic advice column for *The Scottish Daily Record* and regular features for *The Daily Mail*, *Sunday Mirror* and *The People*.

His first book about the psychic genre was published in 1995 and his books are now published in many languages. You can find out more and join Craig & Jane's work and Spiritual Foundation at their website: **psychics.co.uk**

Printed in Great Britain
by Amazon